DISESTABLISHMENT

AND

DISENDOWMENT

OF THE

ENGLISH CHURCH.

VERBATIM REPORT OF THE

TWO NIGHTS' PUBLIC DEBATE

BETWEEN MESSRS.

C. BRADLAUGH AND W. SIMPSON,

*Held at the Concert Hall, Lord Nelson Street, Liverpool,
on July 4th and 5th, 1876.*

CHARLES WATTS, 17, JOHNSON'S COURT, FLEET STREET.

PRICE SIXPENCE.

PAMPHLETS, ETC., BY CHARLES WATTS.

Secularism in its Various Relations, 56 pages	0 6
Merits and Demerits of Secularism. Debate on the above	0 6
Christian Evidences Criticised. The National Secular Society's Reply to the Christian Evidence Society	0 8
The Bible and Christianity	0 6
Origin of Christianity and the Historical Value of the New Testament. Two night's discussion with the Rev. B. H. Cowper.	0 6
Four Nights' Discussion with the Rev. Alex. Stewart, of Aberdeen, on Belief in God and Authenticity of the Four Gospels	1 0
Why am I an Atheist, or Theism Criticised	0 2
Freethought and Modern Progress	0 2
Christianity : its Nature and Influence	0 2
Science and the Bible Antagonistic	0 2
Christian Scheme of Redemption (second edition)	0 1
The Philosophy of Secularism (second edition)	0 1
A Defence of Secular Principles	0 1
The Character of Christ	0 1
Origin of Christianity	0 1
Historical Value of the New Testament	0 1
Miracles	0 1
Prophecies	0 1
The Progress of the Christian Religion	0 1
Practicability of Christianity, and its Influence on Human Conduct	0 1
The Christian Deity	0 1
The Moral Value of the Bible	0 1
Is the Bible Reliable as a Guide ?	0 1
The Christian's Notion of Man's Ultimate State of Existence	0 1
Atheism and Crime	0 ½
National Secular Society's Tracts—No. 5, Secular Teachings. No. 6, Secular Work. Per hundred (post free 1s 2d)	1 0
"Conservative Reaction"	0 1
The English Monarchy and American Republicanism.	0 1
Toryism Tested by the Records of History	0 1
The Government and the People : a Plea for Reform	0 1
Republicanism : Reply to Mr. John Bright	0 1

WORKS BY MRS. ANNIE BESANT.

History of the Great French Revolution. A Course of Six Lectures. Cloth, lettered, 2s 6d ; or in paper covers (May be had in parts—Parts I. to V. 3d. each ; Part VI. 4d.)	2 0
The Secular Song and Hymn Book. Second edition, cloth, gilt	1 0
The Political Status of Women	0 4
Auguste Comte : his Philosophy, his Religion, and his Sociology	0 6
The True Basis of Morality	0 2
Civil and Religious Liberty	0 3
Liberty, Equality, and Fraternity	0 1
Landlords, Tenant Farmers, and Labourers	0 1
Catholicism and Rationalism : a Review of a Two Nights' Discussion between Charles Watts and "A Catholic," held at the Hall of Science, Old Street. With an Essay on the Relative Merits of Secularism and Catholicism.	0 2
The Gospel of Christianity and the Gospel of Freethought	0 2
National Secular Society's Tracts—No. 3, Secular Morality. No. 4, The Bible and Woman. Per hundred (post free 1s 2d)	1 0
Civil and Religious Liberty ; Political Status of Women ; True Basis of Morality ; Landlords, Tenant Farmers, and Labourers; and Liberty, Equality, and Fraternity. Bound in one volume	1 0

London : C. Watts, 17, Johnson's Court, Fleet Street.

DISESTABLISHMENT

AND

DISENDOWMENT

OF THE

ENGLISH CHURCH.

VERBATIM REPORT OF THE

TWO NIGHTS' PUBLIC DEBATE

BETWEEN MESSRS.

C. BRADLAUGH AND W. SIMPSON,

Held at the Concert Hall, Lord Nelson Street, Liverpool
on July 4th and 5th, 1876.

LONDON:
CHARLES WATTS, 17, JOHNSON'S COURT, FLEET STREET.

———

PRICE SIXPENCE.

DISESTABLISHMENT & DISENDOWMENT

OF THE ENGLISH CHURCH.

THIS discussion, between **Mr. William Simpson,** who contested Liverpool in the working man's interest at the general election of 1874, and **Mr. Charles Bradlaugh,** on the subject, "The Disestablishment and Disendowment of the State Church a Political Necessity," created great excitement in Liverpool, and the Concert Hall, Lord Nelson Street, was densely crowded in every corner, many ladies being present. At about a quarter to eight o'clock the two disputants came upon the platform, and were received with loud cheers by their respective supporters, who were apparently present in nearly equal numbers.

Mr. SIMPSON: **As Mr. Bradlaugh and myself are very anxious to keep punctuality with you, we deem it desirable at once to appoint a Chairman, so that when 8 o'clock comes the discussion will at once commence without any delay; and we will close punctually at 10. I, therefore, propose Mr. Joseph Shepherd as Chairman for the night.** (Applause.)

Mr. BRADLAUGH : I have very great pleasure in seconding that motion.

The motion having been put to the meeting, and carried unanimously,

Mr. JOSEPH SHEPHERD took the chair. He said: Ladies and Gentlemen,—The question to be debated to-night is one upon which there is great diversity of opinion, and if the antecedents of the discussion are anything to go by, very strong feeling has from time to time been manifested on the question. As Chairman this evening, I presume that my business will be almost a sinecure. From the amount of intelligence I see before me, I think I shall have no difficulty in keeping the meeting in proper order. (Hear, hear.) You are all aware that the gentlemen who have to handle the question are both of them public men, men well known throughout the length and breadth of the land; and, if you will take my advice as Chairman of this meeting, you will allow the two disputants to be the only two speakers. (Hear, hear, and applause.) My business will be to call them to time. As to the mode in which they shall handle the question, I do not think that is my business at all; neither is it yours much, for, if one of them happens to make a slip the other will be very ready indeed to take advantage of it. (Laughter.) Now, if you will only bear this in mind, you will save me a very great deal of trouble. The manner in which the debate is to be conducted is this: Each gentleman will speak for half an hour to begin with. Mr. Bradlaugh will take the lead. After he has spoken for half an hour Mr. Simpson will speak for half an hour. After that they will speak alternately for 15 minutes each, until 10 o'clock. Now, you will only kindly bear in mind what I have just suggested—that you should leave the subject of debate entirely to the two gentlemen who have it in hand, and allow me merely to call them to time when the time is up, we shall have a very good debate I have no doubt. (Hear, hear.) Having said so much, all that I can tell you now is the subject of the debate. I may just announce to you that a verbatim report of this discussion will be taken and published in the *National Reformer*. Consequently, anyone who wishes to see the report in full will have an opportunity of seeing it in that paper. "The Disestablishment and Disendowment of the Church of England a Political Necessity." That is the question of debate this evening, and I will, without further preface, ask our friend, Mr. Bradlaugh, to occupy the first half hour.

Mr. BRADLAUGH, on rising, was received with cheers. He said: Mr. Chairman, Mr. Simpson, and Friends,—I do not anticipate that in this debate, as far as myself and my opponent are concerned, we shall either of us give you very much cause of special excitement; but the question is, as the Chairman has said, one on which a considerable amount of feeling has already been manifested in different parts of England; and there is the more need, therefore, to appeal to you on both sides to be as judicial as you can. I do not mean that, if you disagree with me, I absolutely object to dissent; and I certainly very much like occasionally to hear applause—(laughter)—but I do mean that, as far as my friends are concerned, nothing should tempt them to hiss my antagonist. (Hear, hear, and applause.) Those who are against me I must leave to exercise their own discretion, only hoping that they will exercise it wisely. I may say that I believe my opponent is as earnest as I claim to be, in his defence of the position he is here to defend—(hear, hear)—and I will ask you, therefore, not to suppose that any language of mine means personal insinuation against my antagonist. The question I have to affirm is this: that the disestablishment and disendowment of the State Church is a political necessity; and I am going to treat that, not as a theological, but as a political, question. I wish at once to say that the utterances from my lips in this debate are not to be put to the account of any others than myself. I do not speak here for the Liberation Society. I have no right to speak for it, and I have no right to commit the Liberation Society by any views I hold. I speak here as a citizen, with the right of a citizen to speak upon a question affecting all citizens, and although in many matters I find myself at one with the Liberation Society, I am not in any fashion a member of that association, nor am I in the slightest correspondence with them or working in any manner with them, except so far as I conceive it to be the duty of all political reformers to try to get rid of what they regard as a blot on our political institutions. (Hear, hear, and "no, no.") Now, I affirm that there ought to be religious equality, that there ought not to be any distinctions made in respect to the opinions or professions of any man, or body of men, on religious matters. I affirm that no man, or body of men, ought to enjoy in a free country any exclusive privileges on account of his or their belonging to any particular Church—(applause)—and that no man, or body of men, ought to suffer any disabilities on account of his or their not conforming to any special Church. (Renewed applause.) That affirmation it will be my duty to maintain to you by a number of arguments. And I am glad to know that here I challenge the very ground taken by the highest authorities of the Church of England; for, in the debate on the disestablishment and disendowment of the Irish Church, the Archbishop of Canterbury distinctly said that he contended against the principle of religious equality; and a little while ago the Bishop of Peterborough said that, as a minister of the Established Church, founded on the principle of religious inequality, he could not make any ostentatious protestations of religion equality. Now, I say that this inequality is political inequality. (No.) I urge that, until you have religious equality affirmed as clearly as it is possible to affirm it, you have not a state of things which ought to obtain in a free country. I submit that, in a state like England, the Church of the majority even ought not to have exclusive privileges, and I will urge upon you further that it is by no means clear that the Established Church is the Church of the majority. Lord Shaftesbury about three years ago in a letter written in his own hand—which was published without his name in the *New York World*, but the original of which I have seen — said he believed that, if the people of England were polled on the question of the establishment or the disestablishment of the English Church, there would be an overwhelming vote in favour of its disestablishment. (Hear, hear, and applause.) At any rate, even as far as England is concerned, the very best that can be said by any advocate of the Established Church is that the established Church is the Church of not a very large majority, and that majority a decreasing one, contending against a very large minority, and that minority an increasing one. (Hear, hear.) But I shall submit to you that the case is even stronger than that. The wails and lamentations of the bishops in their addresses, and of the archdeacons in their visitations—wails and lamentations because the working classes do not attend Church—show that they feel they do not get at the heart of the people ; and I shall submit to you that, as far as England is concerned, the evidence is by no means clear that, reckoning in even everybody who does go to Church, the Church has got a majority, and that, if you leave out those who do not go to Church, and who are only Church of England men because you do not know what they are—(laughter)—and have never reckoned them, then the Church of England is in an overwhelming minority. In Wales it is clear that the Church of England only represents a very small minority of the population, and in Scotland it is also clear that the Established Church is in a minority. But I say that, even if it had a majority, it ought not to have exclusive privileges. I say that, if it is a question of majority, you will find yourself in a very fatal position if you try to argue it. What are you going to argue? That there ought to be an established Church ? What for? For the whole state—for the majority of the citizens of the State ? Then you will have to take in the whole population, home and colonial, including the population of India, in which case you might find a majority of Mahomedans—(laughter) —and I do not suppose that even Mr. Simpson will contend to-night that there ought to be an established Mahomedan Church. (Renewed laughter.) Then I shall submit to you that religion is not the business of the Government at all— (cheers)—that Government should be the best contrivance of national wisdom to provide for national happiness; and that it has neither the duty, nor the right, nor the ability, to select one religious body in preference to any other. (Applause.) We will suppose for a moment the contrary of the proposition. We will suppose that a government has the right. You will get a Premier with the religious views of Mr. Gladstone; you will get a Premier with the views on religion of Mr. Disraeli; I will not call these latter, religious views, because I do not suspect them of being religious views; and I will ask you whether you do not put your-selves in a sad dilemma if you advance the proposition that a government ought in any way to interfere in selecting a religion for the masses. I say the duty of the government is to provide the best education for its citizens—(hear, hear)—and to leave them to find the best religion out of their best judgment. (Hear, hear.) I say that the right position of the government of a free country should be to maintain equal right of worship for all classes of its citizens who desire to worship, to make no invidious dis-tinctions in favour of any, and to impose no disabilities on any form of faith, or on any want of faith; that it should give the most complete protection to those who want a Church, and that it should not put the slightest compulsion on any who do not want it. (Applause.) Then, I shall affirm to you that to make the temporal head of the nation the actual head of one Church out of many in the nation is an invidious declaration in favour of such Church against all others. I will show you a great many other consequences that result from that presently. You make in law, in form, and in legal fact, the Queen the head of the Church, and you make the Queen's representative sitting in the Court of Judicature the interpreter of the doctrine the bishops ought to hold. I submit that the whole of this is utterly wrong; and it drags in with it a difficulty connected with the presence in one of the branches of the legislature of spiritual peers. I say that to give the right to the chiefs of one Church to sit in Parliament only because they are chiefs of that Church is a political inequality of the most outrageous description. (Cheers.) I believe that it is a political inequality which is very fast dying away. I do not suppose that many years will elapse before the bishops will lose their seats in the House of Lords. It is only about 74 years since the House of Commons by its vote excluded the priests of the Church of England from sitting in the House of Commons, and Lord Thurlow then said that if the Bill went to disfranchise the lower orders of the clergy it might go to the length of striking at the reverend bench opposite to him in that House—(hear, hear)—although he said he knew it had been held that the right reverend prelates sat in that House, not as spiritual peers, but by right of their baronies as temporal peers. (Hear, hear.) The gentleman who says "hear, hear" evidently thinks that it is a great point that they are temporal peers. (A Voice from the front seats : "Does the Queen make bishops?") What she does not do is to make sensible men, to sit quiet in the front pew. (Laughter and applause.) I ask, if they sit there by right of their temporal possessions, what temporal possessions have they got? and I answer that the Church of England has no temporal possession that is not the property of the nation. (Hear, hear, and applause.) I shall prove that to you in the course of this debate, or try to; but that is my submission governing it. If they are to sit there as temporal barons, then let them go there as temporal barons ; but they go there as spiritual peers, and I appeal to my friend, who is opposed to me, whether it is not the fact that the presence of the bishops in the House of Lords has been as obstructive of all progress as it is possible to conceive ? (Cheers.) I submit that to make the legal tribunals of the sovereign the interpreters of Church doctrine, and the regulators of Church ceremonies, is manifestly absurd and degrading, and to make the appointment of ecclesiastical dignitaries dependent on the question of whether a Whig or a Tory Premier is in office is unworthy of any Church. (Hear, hear.) A gentleman, anticipating my argument, with that penetrating wisdom which is marked upon his forehead—(laughter)—asked me just this moment whether the Queen made bishops. No, I do not think she does. I believe they are generally the creation resulting from a great deal of intrigue between the Prime Minister and certain peers. I believe that, one time, during Lord Palmerston's term of office, Lord Shaftesbury had a great deal to do with it, and I am not sufficiently in the confidence of Mr. Disraeli to know whether or no he consults the Chief Rabbi of England when he is making an appointment. (Laughter.) All I know is—though the *Congé d'élire* is issued—the writ of right to elect is the veriest sham. (Hear, hear.) What have we had? We had the Dean and Chapter of Hereford some time ago, when Lord John Russell was First Lord of the Treasury, before he was Earl Russell, refusing to appoint a Dr. Hampden, and Lord Russell then wrote back, "I have received your letter, in which you tell me you intend to break the law. Will you disobey the commands of the Queen?" The Church has a perfect right to elect the man whom the Prime Minister selects from amongst her priests, and her right is limited to that. She has Hobson's choice—that or nothing. (Laughter.) Now, I urge to you that the consequences of this become very monstrous; for what do you have? You have the ecclesiastical authorities adjudged incapable of regulating their own affairs, and, whilst any Nonconformist body manages on questions of discipline to regulate those for itself, you have an appeal here to civil tribunals; Sir Henry James briefed on the one side, Mr. Fitzjames Stephen on the other, Mr. Hawkins, Q.C., on the other, and Mr. Serjeant Ballantine on the other, and an attorney on each, with the best Old Bailey knowledge, endeavouring to ascertain the court's decision as to whether a rag may be turned inside or out on the shoulders of preachers, whether it may be red, blue, or green; whether a light may be burned or extinguished, the host elevated or depressed, or what doctrine may be preached. I submit to you that the Church of England is a body deriving from the State a large proportion of its income, so large a proportion that it may be taken as outweighing any objections from those who speak of its voluntary income. I submit to you that its formularies derive their legal authority from the State; I submit to you that Parliament has complete control over it just as over any other association; and I say more than that, that the very prayers and services of the Church of England are subject to alteration by Parliament. I thought I would, in preparation for this debate, make some statement of the laws that had been passed from time to time affecting the Church of England; but I found they were so numerous that it would be utterly impossible to make even a descriptive epitome of the statutes for a two nights' debate. Now, I only put this to you to show you that the Church is an institution with which Parliament may deal, just as it may with a canal or a railroad. The canal may be right; the rail-road may be right; and Parliament may affirm them both. If Parliament thinks them wrong, it has the right to deal with them in contrary fashion. I am going to submit to you that the House of Commons is exactly in that position with regard to the Church; and I say, what an anomaly you have in a State Church, because you have a House of Commons, with Mr. Henry Richard now in it, who is clearly not a Church of England man; with Edward Miall, who was in it, who was clearly not a Church of England man; with John Stuart Mill, who was in it, who was clearly not a Church of England man; with half a dozen Jews now in it, who cannot be suspected of being Church of England men. So that you have the dilemma that, if the Church of England be the State institution I say it is, under the control of Parliament, as I say it is, you have a House of Commons that may possibly have a majority of people not Churchmen in it, to regulate what the Church shall do, and what it shall say in its services. (Cheers.) I submit to you that that is one of the most ridiculous illustrations you can have. That the Church has been regulated by Parliament no one can for a moment doubt. Up to 1677 the Church claimed the right to burn heretics; not only claimed it, but exercised it. I should have stood a very poor chance of mercy at the hands of the Church prior to that date. (Laughter.) Parliament in 1677 took away from the Church that right. Up to 1644 the Church claimed the right to tax herself. In 1664 Parliament took away from the Church that right. I need not tell you how repeatedly, down to that last grand measure which will always form a mighty feature in the life of William Ewart Gladstone—(cheers)—I mean the disestablishment of the Irish Church—(loud cheers)—the right and ability of Parliament to do this has been unquestioned. Now, I will ask you for a moment to look at the Church as a political institution. I will not take you very far back. I do not want to limit Mr. Simpson. I will be prepared to follow him as far back as he likes to go in the history of the Church. I will only at present go as far as Charles II., a virtuous—(laughter)—and pious head of the Established Church. (Laughter.) Well, now, you will find in 1681 the divines of the Church in the strongest way preaching the doctrine of the divine origin and patriarchal descent of the monarch, and the indefeasible hereditary right of the monarch to unquestioning obedience; and as late as 1844 you will find a clergyman of the Church of England——(A Voice: "What is his name?") I wish your name could be Silence. (Laughter.) You will find a clergyman of the Church of England, the Rev. Mr. Sewell, saying "that the reigning prince is a being armed with supreme physical power by the hand and permission of Providence, and, as such, the lord of our property, the master of our lives, the fountain of honour, the dispenser of law, before whom each subject must surrender his will and conform his actions." Now that doctrine is a doctrine common to the Church. We find it supporting James II. on his accession to the throne, despite his vices; and we find that when it turned against him, it was not on account of any of his rascalities, but only because he had issued a declaration which, in some degree, gave toleration to other religious bodies in the State. Now, I am not going to defend James II., but I am going to ask you to look at the Church ——one day affirming James as the head of the Church, affirming the duty of passive obedience to him, and the next day turning against him for another King, because he gave privileges to Nonconformists, which they feared would include Catholics also; they at the time——when I say "they" I mean the members of the Church of England——persecuting Dissenters with a virulence and a bitterness, a cruelty and a malice which seem only to belong to a barbarous age. And then, when they had William III., we find them turning against him because they found that he favoured dissent more than they expected; and we actually find them setting up a lot of opposition bishops, so that for a variety of the sees of the Church for some time you had two sets of bishops, one in opposition to the other. Take again the presence of the bishops in the House of Lords. The Church has no right certainly to claim its peers in the House, because the proper sphere of its work should be its own House of Convocation. Well, what is Convocation? Since 1717 Convocation has been practically dead. It is an establishment where they do nothing but stick little pegs in the pathway of the world to show how far they have *not* gone——(Laughter)——whilst the whole world is marching on. (Applause.) What was the conduct of the Church of England clergy whilst America was struggling against unjust taxation? They went with George III. against the whole of the colonies. A hundred years have gone since then, and in that hundred years the power of the Church for mischief has much decreased. A centennial ring is sounding on the other side to-day, and before another centennial ring gives its echo throughout the world there will be an utter end to this establishment, which I have to impeach to-night. ("Never," and prolonged cheering.) What we ask is that, as in America, all religious bodies shall be on the same footing. (Hear, hear.) The Church has been disestablished in Ireland. Why? Not only because it was the Church of the minority, but because it was a Church which injured progress, because it was a Church which lived on the land and did nought to improve it, because it was a Church which, with the means of education in its hands, did not reach the people, did not aid them, did not raise them. (Interruption.) Why, you can tell what the Church is, when it cannot even keep one quiet whilst the multitude are silent. (Applause.) I have only one minute and, therefore, shall not occupy your time longer at this point. I shall go through my case in this way. I am sure my opponent will do me the justice to say that there has not been the shadow of a personal allusion ; and I hope that in that fashion this debate may go on. (Cheers.)

The CHAIRMAN : Mr. Simpson will occupy the next half hour. (A Voice : "Three cheers for the Church !" and cheers.)

Mr. SIMPSON : Mr. Chairman, Mr. Bradlaugh, Ladies, and Gentlemen,—I reciprocate Mr. Bradlaugh's last language. I hope that Mr. Bradlaugh will continue this debate just as he has begun it, because, if he does, the side that I have to espouse will receive no hurt. (Hear, hear.) If Mr. Bradlaugh is to suppose for one single moment that he is addressing an audience that is to be carried away by his peculiar fire and his peculiar energy—(applause)—and his peculiar emphasis, and that all the points he has submitted, that he is going to deal with in the course of two nights, you are to take for granted contain some immense fact, and he does no more than that, why I quite endorse his last expression, and say I hope that, as the discussion has commenced, so it will be carried on. Mr. Bradlaugh has made one or two appeals to me during his address to you, and I think he will not object if I make one or two to him. (A Voice: "No personalities.") No; I am not guilty of personalities. (A man, who had been noisy during Mr. Bradlaugh's speech, here interrupted again.)

Mr. BRADLAUGH: This stupid man seems to interrupt both sides in partially.

Mr. SIMPSON: Yes, and that is the way in which I want the debate to be carried on. I ask Mr. Bradlaugh if he thinks, with all his practice as a debater, that one man can reply to the numerous points he has raised in his thirty minutes' address? Whilst I make this remark, I make this declaration, that he has not given one single particle of argument on the question to be debated. (Applause.) And, mind you, Mr. Bradlaugh has got to prove his position, that to disestablish and disendow the Church of England is a present political necessity. (Applause.) I am not here, and I trust Mr. Bradlaugh will not suppose I have come here, for the purpose of defending all that has been done by certain sons of the Church, either since the time of Charles I., or before the time of Charles I. (Hear, hear.) I am here to-night simply to say: "You, Mr. Bradlaugh, contend that the Church ought to be disestablished and disendowed; and I am here to show that your arguments, if you have any, are not sound in their basis on that point." (Cheers.) There is not an institution under heaven that I know of—and I think I may venture to state that there is not one that Mr. Bradlaugh knows of, much as he knows—but, if you were to rake it all up from its commencement to the present time, it would look an awful failure. Take any institution—and I say this with not the slightest desire to wound our friend—take any institution you think proper, and, from its commencement up to the present time, there will be found that in it which no sane man would attempt to defend. That is not the question. The question we have to debate is, not whether the bishops, during the time of Charles I., did this, or whether they did not; whether they voted for James one day, and then voted for somebody else against James the next day: that is not the question. The question is, "The Church of England, as she now exists, as she stands before us to-day; is it a political necessity that you should disestablish and disendow her?" (Cries of "Yes," "No," and cheers.) I think some of my friends do not understand it. That is the question we are met to discuss. There is no doubt about it; and, if you have come to hear any other question, you have made a

mistake, and you had better go out. My friend, Mr. Bradlaugh, has evidently made a mistake. He has not got at
the right question, that is quite certain, because he commenced by telling us that he was not quite certain whether
the Church was in a majority or a minority. The idea of
a gentleman coming all the way from London to discuss
this question ! (Laughter and applause.) Aye, and we
are to take two nights over it. (Renewed laughter.) And,
what is more, he has actually come down to Liverpool for
me to tell him whether she is or she is not.

Mr. BRADLAUGH : Hear, hear.

Mr. SIMPSON : Mr. Bradlaugh says "hear, hear." I
think it is a very natural assumption for me to say that a
gentleman who comes so far, who is so well up in all and
everything connected with public speaking and debating—
(cries of " Question," and " Keep to the argument.")

The CHAIRMAN : I hope all the friends of Mr. Bradlaugh,
at any rate, will give Mr. Simpson the same sort of hearing
that Mr. Bradlaugh had.

Mr. BRADLAUGH : Let me add to what the Chairman has
said, that I have not heard Mr. Simpson away from the
question as yet. It is his fashion to deal with it as I do,
and it is your duty to allow him to speak. (A Voice : " He
shouldn't be personal.") Never mind ; leave that to me.

Mr. SIMPSON : I am exceedingly anxious to please all
here in the mode of dealing with this question ; but, whilst
I am anxious to do that, I must follow what I conceive to
be the rights of this question from my intellectual stand-
point. I contend that I am not dealing in personalities,
and I appeal to my friend, Mr. Bradlaugh. It is his own
language—that he is not certain whether the Church is in
a minority or in a majority. Now, I contend, without personality, that the first thing I would have done, had I been
Mr. Bradlaugh, would have been to look up for statistics,
and try to make myself master of that position at any rate.
True, some difficulty might have arisen : he would have
found one statistician say one thing, and another another ;
but he could have done with them, as he could with everything else, in the might of his own intellectual force—
jumbled it up, and thrown it at you, and said something
about it one way or the other. But he does not ; he says,
" I do not know." Well, gentlemen, I do know, and, not
to trouble you with the dry details of figures to fractions—
I shall be happy to pass figures to Mr. Bradlaugh, if he

wishes it—I tell you that the Church of England is in a majority of two millions over all the sects in this country. (Cheers.) If you want my authority, my authority is a Dissenter, not a member of the Church of England, and one, I think, that Mr. Bradlaugh will not dispute. His name is Mann, a celebrated man in figures. (Laughter.) I do not know anybody that has ever yet attempted to dispute the figures that gentleman has given on the question we are at present considering. Now, ladies and gentlemen, bear in mind that, in round numbers, he states that the Church of England worshippers are in excess of every other sect by two millions, or thereabouts. Now mark, ladies and gentlemen, what does that mean? It does not mean, even suppose you grant the whole two millions, and nothing more than that—it does not mean that there is in the balance against the Church—that is to say, in the Nonconformist bodies—that, because they nonconform, they go in for disestablishment and disendowment. Why, what does Mr. Rogers say? What does Mr. Dale say in London? At the last conference held these two gentlemen, who stumped the whole country for disestablishment and disendowment, reported that their tour through the country had been a failure. (Hear, hear.) That is the language of the Rev. Mr. Rogers. (A Voice: "No; it is not.") It is not my language; and, mind you, they are two Dissenting ministers, going about the country on purpose to agitate this question, and their evidence is that their mission throughout the country of England has been a failure. Now, what are they going to try to do? They are going into Scotland to see whether they can make a better fight of it there than they have made here in England; and, I suppose, when they have finished there, if they do not succeed to their heart's content, they will go into Wales; and, if they do not succeed there, perhaps they will go to Ireland, and see what they can do there. So far as England is concerned, the evidence of these gentlemen is that their mission has been a failure. What does that mean? It means this, that Nonconformists are not in favour of disestablishment and disendowment as a rule; that it is only the exception where even a Nonconformist is in favour of disestablishment and disendowment. Well, ladies and gentlemen, if you take those belonging to Nonconformist bodies who are against disestablishment and disendowment, and you add their numbers to the numbers in excess that the Church has over every other denomination, you have a fact which at once must teach my friend, Mr. Bradlaugh, that upon this question, not only is the Church in a majority, but that the whole country is in a majority against disestablishment and disendowment. (Cheers.) I have already told you that it is impossible to follow Mr. Bradlaugh through all the points brought forward in the thirty minutes he has occupied, and I can only just point out one here and there. Mr. Bradlaugh made a pleasing hit, I grant it—one of those kind of hits which is bound to find its way to every Englishman's heart. "I submit," said Mr. Bradlaugh, "that there ought to be religious equality." (Hear, hear, and cheers) Well, who says there ought not? (Hear, hear.) I do not. I have advocated religious equality ever since I can remember; but we are not here to-night to discuss the question of religious equality. We are here to-night for the purpose of discussing whether the Church ought to be disestablished and disendowed, and as a reason for this Mr. Bradlaugh ought to give some evidence to show that there is no religious equality in her existence. If that could be shown, I grant now that it would be a point in the argument; but simply to state, "I submit that there ought to be religious equality," is not an argument: it is a simple, pleasing mode of a man expressing a truism, which every honest heart ought to echo. Nothing more nor less. But where is there the inequality about the Church of England? I do not know of any? Mr. Bradlaugh blows hot and cold with one breath in this matter. He grumbles, first of all, that there is no religious equality, and then what does he tell you? He tells you that you can almost talk anything you like, and be a member of the Church of England; you can preach any doctrine you like, and be a member of the Church of England; you can either have candles or no candles—(laughter)—you can have either a night-dress or a flannel jacket—it does not matter which. (Renewed laughter) So much religious equality is there in the Church that she actually allows her ministers to do almost anything at all they like. But what is it? Is it not nonsense—for our friend, Mr. Bradlaugh, at any rate—to talk about equality? I ask him. Is it possible to obtain equality of any kind, under any circumstances? (Hear, hear.) Is it not simply a word conventionally conveying a certain idea after this fashion—removing obstructions out of every man's way, and giving him free access equal with his fellows? That is the only equality we can have in this world ; we can have no other. Well, does not that exist in the Church of England? I can go to church if I like, and I can stop away if I like. Cannot you? (Hear, hear, and laughter.) Cannot you go to a Methodist chapel if you like, or a Presbyterian chapel? There is no Church law which inflicts upon you pains and penalties if you do not go. (A Voice : "There used to be.") Allow me. This, Mr. Bradlaugh has told you, is a political question, and not a religious one ; and I submit that, though there may be, religiously considered, pains and penalties in the Church of England, politically considered, there is perfect equality in her existence. I know it is a favourite idea with all who take Mr. Bradlaugh's side of the question we are now discussing, that religion ought to be equal. I know it ought, and I submit that anything more equal than the conduct of the Church towards the citizens of this country my mind cannot conceive. I can either go to church, or stop away from church; I can be a Baptist to-day, a Mormon or Mahomedan the next day ; and there are no political pains and penalties attached to me for so doing. (Cheers) Then for Mr. Bradlaugh simply to say to you that he believes in religious equality is simply to utter a pleasing sentiment ; but does not touch the question the consideration of which we have met to debate. The question we have met to debate is this : Is there in the Church's existence some particular action of so unequal a character as to make it a necessity that she ought to be disestablished and disendowed? (A Voice : "No.") Now, then, if Mr. Bradlaugh can prove that point, it is one point in his favour, and no one would be more ready than myself to admit that he has scored one ; but that has got to be done yet. (Cheers.) "No body of men ought to enjoy any privilege over any other citizens." (Hear, hear.) I think that was Mr. Bradlaugh's language. He will pardon me if I happen to make a little mistake, because it is hard work for a gentleman to write in long-hand what another is speaking. That is the idea at all events. Well, I say the same. (Laughter.) I would like to see it if we were every one co-equal with the other—that I had as much as you, and you as much as me, and so on. (Laughter.) I would like to see that, but I do not hope I shall ever see it; and supposing I should hope to see it, is that any reason why we should disestablish and disendow the Church ? Because we are not all as rich, one man as another? Because I am Lord Derby, and my friend *not* Lord Shaftesbury—(laughter)—is that any reason why the Church of England should be disestablished and disendowed? I submit to you, ladies and gentlemen, that that is no reason for disestablishment and disendowment of the Church, because in society there is no general political equality. (Cheers.) Ah! but Mr. Bradlaugh thought, a little further on, that the Church of England was in an immense minority. You (to Mr. Bradlaugh) remember it, no doubt.

Mr. BRADLAUGH : Yes, yes.

Mr. SIMPSON : First, he did not know whether she was in a minority or not, but five minutes afterwards he was morally certain that she was in an immense minority. (Laughter and cheers.) Inspiration comes quick to some public speakers, does it not? (Renewed laughter.) Facts soon give way in the minds of some philosophers, before evidence we know nothing at all about. But Mr. Bradlaugh gave us no evidence whatever even of his second thought on the question—no evidence whatever, and I submit that, until we have the evidence that she is in the minority, I have a right to claim that that portion of his subject has not been made good. (Cheers.) But, ladies and gentlemen, for a moment, while I think of it, supposing she was in a minority—let us suppose that instead of numbering, for example, nine millions as against seven, or seven millions rather as against nine—supposing the Church only numbered seven millions, and all the rest of the sects numbered nine, would that be any reason for disestablishing and disendowing her? ("Yes" and "No.") Would it? mind what you are saying. Mr. Bradlaugh would not say that, because, if that be a reason for disestablishment and disendowment, then the fact that she is in a majority, instead of a minority, must be a reason why she should not be disestablished and disendowed. (Cheers.) I submit to you, ladies and gentlemen, that this absolutely is not the question—which of the Churches is in the majority ; we have not come here to discuss that question. True, it may be advanced in the course of the debate as a matter of argument, but we are not here to discuss it. I submit, with all respect to you, that the question of figures has nothing to do absolutely with the question we are brought together to discuss to-night. However great may be her minority her influence may be so great to our country's good that to disestablish and disendow her might be a permanent injury instead of a blessing. (Cheers.) I submit that. Therefore, I say, ladies and gentlemen, that whether Mr. Bradlaugh's figures as he may give them to us just now, or mine, be correct, that does not touch the question at issue. The question is, Is it a political necessity that she should be disestablished and disendowed? That Mr. Bradlaugh has got to prove. So far, I think, you will agree with me he has not done it. (Cheers.) Then Mr. Bradlaugh told us that religion was not the business of a Government. Well, whoever said it was? I am not here to say that it is, or that it was, or that it will be, or that it ought to be. I draw your attention to these things, ladies and gentlemen, because I do not want your minds to be led astray by them. Do not be carried away by his pleasing style, and the warm manner in which he sets things before you. (Laughter and Cheers.) I quite agree with him at once, so that we may understand each other the first night. I quite agree with him that religion is not the business of the Government; in other words, that the Government has no right to interfere with religion. I quite agree with him; but that is not the question here to night. (A Voice: "Yes it is.") No, pardon me, it is not. I know the question, and I respectfully submit that, even if I admit it, Mr. Bradlaugh has not shown you that the Government in any way interferes with the religion of the Church of England. ("Oh, oh," and cheers.) I will tell you what he has done, for you do not know, some of you: he has shown you that the Government has interfered with the existence of the Church as a political institution. That he has done, but he has given you no evidence so far that the Government interferes with the Church in her religious capacity. (Cheers.) The object I have in coming here to debate with Mr. Bradlaugh is to show, if I possibly can, how empty and hollow are the statements made by gentlemen who take the same side of this question that Mr. Bradlaugh is taking, and if you will note the difference I have just pointed out to you, you will see that all Mr. Bradlaugh's illustrations on the conduct of Parliament towards the Church so far given by him to-night, have reference to her existence more as a political institution than any other thing. (Hear, hear.) But he went on and told us a little further that Parliament has a perfect right to do certain things to the Church. I do not say Parliament has not. I will go a step further and say that

Parliament has a right to do anything it likes, no matter what. (" Oh! oh!") That is to say. (" Oh!") Oh! yes; let me understand the question. I say Parliament has a right to do whatever it likes, I do not care what. It has the right thus: it possesses an amount of power which gives it the right. It can take away my right to stand here and address you to-night. (A Voice: "It cannot.") Pardon me, but it can. ("No, no;" and "Yes, yes.") What is the use of you gentlemen saying "No, no," when you are only assembled here to-night and listening to Mr. Bradlaugh and myself under an Act of Parliament. Mr. Bradlaugh will bear me out that, so far as the power of Parliament is concerned, I know no end to its power; excepting, ladies and gentlemen, we bring in one idea. The moment we bring in another idea, then we do curtail the power of Parliament—the right, rather, of Parliament—that is, when we bring in the moral right, when we say Parliament has no right to do that which is not right. When we say that, then we have said all that we can say; but, as far as the political constitution of the House of Commons is concerned, I know no end to the Parliament's right. It is only when it is guarded, when it is curtailed, when it is directed by moral force, that there is a bound put to the Parliamentary action of right. That being so, that being my opinion, I agree with Mr. Bradlaugh that Parliament can disestablish and disendow the Church of England if it likes. But, mind you, the Parliament would have to answer to the people if it did it. (Applause.) Do not forget that. It would have to answer to the people; and when it went to the people, that is to say, when the Members of Parliament went back to their constituencies, having done this vile act, they would have to answer to the majority of the people of England for what they had done—(cheers)—and that majority would send back a new Parliament, and the new Parliament would undo the villainous action of the old. (Cheers.) Mr. Bradlaugh shakes his head; and I will tell you why. Because, amongst his many other great qualifications, he has ventured to do what I never knew him to do before—he has ventured to turn prophet; but he has been as careful as no one but a Bradlaugh could be that neither you nor I will be alive to see whether his prophecy is carried out. (Laughter.) And why? Because he took the precaution of telling us that we will have to wait one hundred years. (Laughter.) It is his own language, ladies and gentlemen. (A Voice: "Time.") Alluding to the centennial celebration in America, he said : "In another hundred years this thing will not be." But "the Government has no right to select one religious denomination from any other religious denomination." I do not know how Mr. Bradlaugh is using this word "right." Sometimes he is using it in a political sense; evidently, at other times he is using it in a moral sense. If he is using it in a moral sense, it would be opening up an immense field both to him and me in this discussion; if he is using it in a political sense—and he told you at the beginning that he was going to treat this question in a political sense—then I say Government has a right to select one form of worship over another. (Cries of "No, no.") What is the use of your being so insane as to say "no" when not only do they possess the right, but they actually carry out their right? The facts are against you. I say, ladies and gentlemen, that politically they do possess the right, and from Mr. Bradlaugh's point of view they exercise that right, but not from my point of view. (A Voice: "Time.") That is very unfair and unkind for any gentleman to call time, when you yourselves have appointed a chairman to call time. I say that the Government has not made a selection of the Church of England, for the Church of England was before the Government was —(cheers)—and, as the Church of England was before the Government was, the Government had no hand in the selection—not the slightest. If Mr. Bradlaugh disputes my affirmation, I shall be prepared to-morrow night to give chapter and verse for the statements I have now made. But he has taken his own position. I contend, that the Government not only possesses the right, but, politically considered, it exercises that right. Then, the Church has been regulated by Parliament, Mr. Bradlaugh says. In much of her conduct I am not prepared to dispute that, because I have already told you that the Parliament has power to do anything. But to the question, before my half hour is up. After all my admissions in harmony with Mr. Bradlaugh, what has it got to do with disestablishment and disendowment? because I am bound, ladies and gentlemen, to keep before our minds the question. The question is that the disestablishment and disendowment of the Church of England is a political necessity; and everything that Mr. Bradlaugh urges ought to be urged with a view to show you that that political necessity exists, and consequently that disestablishment and disendowment ought to follow. (Cheers).

The CHAIRMAN : Mr. Bradlaugh will now occupy the next fifteen minutes.

Mr. BRADLAUGH : I avow that I am a little disappointed with the conduct of the audience during my friend's speech. If you think any of his speech not proper, leave it to me : it can do no good, except to prevent me from understanding what he says, to interrupt whilst he is speaking. And I am still more grieved that, having appointed your own Chairman, you should call "time." You ought to have remembered that your own interruptions compelled the Chairman, in fairness, to give my opponent a longer time, to make allowance for those interruptions. Now, Mr. Simpson has chosen to adopt a style of argument which I have no doubt he thinks thoroughly effective. He must not think me discourteous if I do not choose to follow him in it. I will not hope, or try, to compete with him in fun, because I have so much graver matter to lay before you in these two nights. (Hear, hear.) He says that it is not possible to answer in two nights all the points I raised in my first speech, and he also says there was not a tittle of argument in any of them. One of those statements answers the other : I do not know which is supposed to be most accurate. (Laughter.) He says—and I am sure he would not wish to misrepresent me—that I told him that I was not certain whether or not the Church of England was in a majority, and that five minutes afterwards I discovered suddenly, by inspiration—(laughter)—that she was in an overwhelming minority. I thought I said that the advocates of the Church themselves had not made statements which would enable me to determine whether the Church was in a majority or not ; that, at best, all that could be said for her was that she had a very narrow and decreasing majority, in face of a large and increasing minority—(hear, hear)—and that, if you reckoned in your calculation the population that did not attend church at all, then you had the Church of England in an overwhelming minority. (Cheers.) I keep a memory, and I try to say what I mean. Now, Mr. Simpson has been good enough to quote from a Dissenter. All Dissenters are not infallible ; but one of the most accurate he could quote from is Horace Mann, in connection with the Census Reports ;

and Mr. Simpson only omitted two things. One was to tell you that he was quoting from the Census Report of 1851, and the next was that Horace Mann only reckons as Church of England people 7,546,948, and that he reckons as those who are not Church of England people 10,380,661. (Cheers.) How that makes the Church people 2,000,000 more than all others is, I allow, a problem in arithmetic that I am not capable of solving. (Laughter.) I am bound to say that Mr. Simpson was thoroughly frank. He handed me his figures. I knew what they were, but I wanted to add them up in the best way I could. He did not intend to deceive me, I am quite sure; only the effect of his Church teaching had slightly embarrassed his calculations. (Laughter and cheers.) Now, I shall submit to you that, in addition to there being a majority against the Church in 1851 of 3,233,613*—I think those are the figures, but I may have made a mistake too, so if you like to check me you can—in addition to that, I say that in the twenty-five years that have gone since, the Church has not gained ground. And I say more. I say that in the 7,546,948 that you reckon as Church of England people even in 1851, you get a number of nominal reckonings which are not really live reckonings at all. But I am content to take it on Mr. Simpson's own figures. I do not mean his imaginary figures, but the figures he was good enough to hand to me. (Laughter.) I am content to take it that in 1851 there were 7,546,948 Church of England people, and 10,380,661 who were not. Then I say that in the last ten years the thing that has been more noticeable than anything, is the fact that the bishops have been lamenting that the people stay away from church; and they have been holding conferences in various towns, and services in theatres, and all things of that kind, in order to get the masses there, because they could not get them to come to the churches. So that, clearly, according to Mr. Simpson's own statistics, the Church of England was three millions and a quarter behind, in round figures, twenty-five years ago, and it must be a great many more thousands behind now, or the Church would not wail and lament so every day of the week, and in every address it issues. Now, I am not here to defend Mr. Dale, or Mr. Rogers, and I have not in my mind the particular speeches that Mr. Simpson refers to, when he says

---

* Should be 2,833,713.

they admitted that their tour was a failure; but if his judgment on their speech is not more accurate than his calculation of his own figures, he must pardon me if I take his criticism with a grain of salt. (Laughter.) I can understand that a tour may be a failure, because, for example, a Disestablishment meeting might have been held, say, in a quiet, well-behaved, intellectual Church of England borough, like Liverpool—(laughter)—and that meeting might have been a failure. I can understand that that meeting might have been a failure, without any argument in favour of the Establishment arising from it. It might simply have been a failure because a few people, instead of arguing for the Church, fought for it—imagined that they belonged to the Church militant, without any commission warranting them for it; and I think it would be as well to read the whole of the Rev. Mr. Dale's speech, and the whole of the Rev. Mr. Rogers's speech, if an argument is to be deduced from them in favour of the Establishment. Then Mr. Simpson says that he agrees with me on religious equality; and he says: "Who said there ought not to be religious equality?" The Archbishop of Canterbury. (Hear, hear.) The Bishop of Peterborough. (A Voice: "Proof, proof.") If the indecent Church of England man behind—("Proof, proof")—if the indecent Church of England man up there (pointing to the gallery, where a stout man was loudly shouting "Proof")—who has gone suddenly mad will try to keep silence, he shall have the proof he wants. (Hear, hear.) The Archbishop of Canterbury said so, in the debate in the House of Lords on the disestablishment of the Irish Church. He said: "My Lords, The principle we have to contend against here is the principle of religious equality;" and the Bishop of Peterborough, only a very little while ago said that, as a minister of the Established Church, founded on the principle of religious inequality, he could not make ostentatious proclamation of religious equality. (Cheers.) Mr. Simpson says that the proposition of religious equality is only a truism, which all honest men ought to echo. I agree in that. Then we are both agreed that the Bishop of Peterborough and the Archbishop of Canterbury are not honest men. (Laughter and cheers.) Then Mr. Simpson says "that there are no pains and penalties attending the Church of England Establishment. He can go, or he can stop away. Yes; but they take their pay whether you go or whether you stay away. (Laughter.) Are there no pains and penalties? (A Voice: "No.") Is there not a statute 9 and 10 William III., chapter 32? Under that statute, was not Lord Amberley's will set aside the other day? Does not that statute enact that every person educated in the Christian faith shall be obliged to admit the Thirty-nine Articles? Was not a Church of England clergyman, the Rev. Mr. Coll, deprived of a trusteeship because he did not so admit them? What is the use of telling me there are no pains and penalties? (Cheers.) But then Mr. Simpson says, will I pardon him if he sometimes makes a little mistake? My whole sentiment is of pardon for his speech from beginning to end. (Laughter.) When he answered as he did about equality, there was no such proposition made by me as that to which he directed his answer. My proposition always involved the inequality connected with the Church Establishment; it had nothing to do with equality of property otherwise; it had nothing to do with social condition otherwise. Now, Mr. Simpson asks whether, supposing that the Church of England, instead of being in a majority of 2,000,000—which it is not—were in a minority of 2,000,000, that would be a reason for disestablishing her. Yes. (A Voice: "Prove it," and cries of "Turn him out.") I think you had better let him be; we may make a Nonconformist of him directly. (Laughter.) He is one of the props of the Church and you can see what rotten ones they are. (Laughter and cheers.) Yes, it would be a reason for disestablishing the Church if it were in a minority, for the Church of a minority would have no right to use national property for purposes of which the majority did not get the benefit. (Hear, hear.) Then, Mr. Simpson says: "Who ever said that religion was or ought to be the business of a Government?" But, if religion ought not to be the business of a Government, then the Government should not enforce laws which protect one form of religion against others. "Well, but," says Mr. Simpson, "they do not, because Parliament never interferes in any religious capacity." What is the Public Worship Act but an interference in a religious capacity? (Hear, hear.) We do not seem to know the meaning of language. What is the decision of the Judicial Committee of the Privy Council in half a score of cases? If these are not interferences in religious capacities, then language has no meaning at all. Then he says I told you you would have to wait a hundred years for disestablishment. I said nothing of the sort. I said that before the centennial ring echoed again through the world this Establishment would have disappeared from amongst you. (Cheers.)

Mr. SIMPSON: Now, ladies and gentlemen, we are getting to close quarters, and, if you will be patient, I feel morally certain you will not be disappointed on this question at last. I deeply regret to say that I think my friend, Mr. Bradlaugh, has not dealt fairly with me in his last sentence. (Oh, oh, and Order.) He told you he was not certain whether the Church was in a majority or a minority (A Voice: " Nothing of the kind.") I emphatically declare, and he has not denied it, that that was his first statement. I have given him the figures, and he acknowledged my courtesy in handing him the authority from whence those figures were collected, and he admitted that it was an authority; but he told you that I had made a mistake of three millions as against myself.

Mr. BRADLAUGH: Five millions.

Mr. SIMPSON: *Five* millions?

Mr. BRADLAUGH: Yes.

Mr. SIMPSON: Dear me! Will you, ladies and gentlemen, kindly take out your pencils if you please. Take them out, and, if you please—you that can do so conveniently—(cries of " Go on.") Pardon me, let me do it in my own way, if you please; let us do the thing after our own fashion; and I say to you, ladies and gentlemen, put the figures down as I give them to you, and then you will be the judges between Mr. Bradlaugh and myself. This is the book, Mr. Bradlaugh, from which I quoted, and from which you quoted, accepting my figures.

Mr. BRADLAUGH: Hear, hear.

Mr. SIMPSON: Now then, ladies and gentlemen, I will read for you: Church of England people, 7,546,948; Roman Catholics, 610,786; Protestant Dissenters, and others—(A Voice: " Babies?") No, Sir, you are not counted. (Great laughter.) Protestant Dissenters, and others, with my friend not counted—(renewed laughter)—5,303,609. Now, will you kindly add the two latter figures together, and deduct them from the former, and tell me how far was I off when I said two millions? Do it for yourselves, will you? (A Voice: " Give us them again.") Give you the last figures again? Very well; the last figures are 5,303,609. Now add the two last lots of figures together, and deduct them from the former figures, and you have an excess of

two millions of Churchmen over every other body of subjects. (Cheers.) I give my friend credit—I know he is a
smart man—(laughter.) I offered a £20 note to somebody else to come here and take my place to-night. I was
so frightened of him—(laughter)—not frightened of being
able to maintain my question, ladies and gentlemen, but
afraid of all that cultivated artifice of which my friend is
master. I will show you how he has made his mistake.
Mind you, he told you I made the mistake, but he did not
show you how I had done it; but I will show you how he
has made the mistake. Previous to doing so, I must repeat
my language that the Church of England is in excess of
all other denominations by two millions or thereabouts.
(A Voice: "What is the date of that paper?")

Mr. BRADLAUGH: I rise to order. The original statement in Mr. Simpson's first speech was, as the reporter's
notes will show, that the Church of England was in a
majority of two millions over all other bodies. The word
"Christian" bodies or "denominational" bodies was added
lately.

Mr. SIMPSON: Now, do you not think I had good cause
to be frightened of such an antagonist? (Laughter.) We are
here discussing a question affecting religious bodies especially. (A Voice: "No.") When I quoted the Church of
England, I quoted the numbers of a religious body; when
I used the words, "other bodies," I meant other bodies of
professing Christians. (Oh, oh.) You do not suppose for
one single moment that I would class with "other bodies"
those who profess no religion. (Oh, and Question.) But,
if I mistake not—and bear in mind, if it is to come to the
expression of a single word, I am willing to take the report
—my language was "other sects." (Hear, hear.) Now,
then, I say that other sects must, per necessity, mean other
professing Christian bodies. (Hear, hear.)

Mr. BRADLAUGH: No.

MR. SIMPSON: Mr. Bradlaugh says "No." Very well;
stop a moment, and, if it is trickery, we will have it.
(Cheers, and cries of "Shame.") My language, I contend
—and you that will take the trouble to buy the report from
Mr. Bradlaugh's own newspaper, I think, will find I am
correct in saying so—my language was "other sects." Now,
then, ladies and gentlemen, I appeal to your honest intelligence, when I used the words, "other sects," did not you
take me to mean other sects of Christians? (Cries of

"Yes" and "No.") Now, then, I will show you how Mr. Bradlaugh has made the mistake. Mr. Bradlaugh has made the mistake because he has added to the figures I have already given you, 4,466,266 non-worshipping people. (Ironical Cheers.) Non-worshippers! Now, Nonconformity cannot claim non-worshippers; neither Presbyterians, Baptists, nor anybody else, can claim non-worshippers--(hear, hear)--and my language was, that the Church of England was in excess of all the sects by two millions. So much, then, for Mr. Bradlaugh's correction of me. I contend that he has accepted my figures, and, having accepted the figures I put in his hand, my statement is true, that the Church of England is in excess of other sects by two millions. Very well; now, then, for the argument. Mr. Bradlaugh says, if she is in a minority of two millions, she ought to be disestablished and disendowed, because a minority-Church has no right to handle the property of the majority.

Mr. BRADLAUGH : That was not what I said.

Mr. SIMPSON : Well, then, in substance.

Mr. BRADLAUGH : No; I said—(cries of "Sit down.") Will you allow me to explain?

Mr. SIMPSON : I have no objection.

The CHAIRMAN : Mr. Simpson has no objection to hear an explanation.

Mr. SIMPSON : I think it is only right and fair. I am speaking from memory, and I may have misrepresented Mr. Bradlaugh; and, if so, I am anxious to be put right.

Mr. BRADLAUGH : If an absolute misrepresentation of language takes place—I do not say an intentional misrepresentation—either disputant ought to have a right to rise and correct it. (Hear, hear.) My statement was, that if a Church was in a minority of two millions, the minority ought not to have a right to apply the national property against the wishes of the majority.

Mr. SIMPSON : Well, that is exactly what I said. (Oh, oh, and cheers.) However, if you think it is not, then I will say now that I accept the correction. Now, then, listen to my argument. Then the majority has a perfect right to use National Church property in opposition to the wishes and will of the minority. That must be the obverse argument to the one Mr. Bradlaugh used. But I take exception, because he is assuming that the Church property is national property. (Hear, hear.) It is no such thing. It is public property, but it is not national property. There is a vast deal of difference between them. But Mr. Bradlaugh took another exception : he said I was short of some knowledge, and some information—that I went a long way back for my figures, that I went to 1851. But that is further than he went. He came here and told you he knew nothing at all about it. I did take the trouble to go to 1851 for my figures, but he did not. I will tell you why I went to 1851, because I went as far back as there are any figures to be got ; for there is no statistical account of this description since the year 1851, and I will tell you why. There is not, because the Nonconformist bodies would not permit it. (Cheers.) Mr. Bradlaugh has told you, in his usual kind, amiable, mild, and gentle style, full of knowledge, that the Church is decreasing in numbers, and that Nonconformity is increasing. Bring up the proofs, Mr. Bradlaugh. (Hear, hear.) There has not, ladies and gentlemen, I affirm, been a single statistic of a reliable character printed since 1851 ; and I put it to your reason whether, if I give you the latest figures, and my friend accepts them, he is not bound by them, and if he has no other figures than these, you, ladies and gentlemen, must judge between us in this question. (A Voice : "So we will," and laughter.) I say then, ladies and gentlemen, that the Church is in a majority; but even if she were in a minority, that would be no reason for disestablishing and disendowing her. "No pains and penalties !" says Mr. Bradlaugh. "Oh," and his keen eye flashed round —(laughter)—"no pains and penalties !" and I thought he was going to give us something startling in the shape of pains and penalties ; but he did not—not one word as to political pains and penalties, because I drew the line in my speech. I said that I could go where I liked to worship, and you could go where you liked to worship, and there were no political pains or penalties. (Hear, hear.) Has Mr. Bradlaugh given you any evidence other than that ? ("Yes" and "No.") Yes, he has ; of course he has ; but he gave you a pain and penalty to which my language had no reference—a pain and penalty that I would have to submit to if I belonged to Mr. Bradlaugh's Church—(laughter) —and it is this : if you belonged to the Church, that is to say, if you ally yourself to the Church, become a minister in her communion, you sign a declaration of fealty to certain rules and regulations—you are free to do it—or you are free to leave it alone—(hear)—but once having done that you are in honour bound to observe it. (Cheers.) If you do not observe it the penalty is that they try to kick you out. (Laughter.) Well, is not that right? Is not all society built upon that? If you, ladies and gentlemen, that are here, do but behave yourselves up to the end of our debate, as you have hitherto, we shall be delighted with you, but if you become cantankerous and noisy, and disobey good order, we shall have some of you put out. (Laughter.) It is the pain and penalty of your coming here, and you knew it when you came, and you are bound in honour to behave as men and educated human beings. I say, if I became one of Mr. Bradlaugh's Church—(laughter)—I should be bound with certain rules and regulations, and if I did not obey those rules and regulations i would not be acknowledged as a member of his community. I will go a step further myself. That there are penalties attached to the non-observance of certain views taken I am free to admit, but, ladies and gentlemen, the Church, in her grand entirety, acting as she does on the whole people of this country, inflicts neither pains nor penalties upon any one single man within these realms. That is my affirmation, and that I contend Mr. Bradlaugh has not for one moment disturbed, and as he has not disturbed it, I fail to see so far the necessity of either disestablishing or disendowing the Church. (Cheers, and cries of " Time.") Now, there is your Chairman—

The CHAIRMAN : Order, please.

Mr. SIMPSON : Mr. Bradlaugh was not satisfied with my notion of equality. Well, why did he not give us his own? If he is not satisfied with mine, why does he not give us something else in return for it? I told you—and I felt morally certain he would not dispute with me—that equality other than that I described is a perfect impossibility. You can only have equality of a political character, after the fashion of removing obstructions between one man and another man—(hear, hear)—and then you are not equal. Are Mr. Bradlaugh and I equal? (Cries of " No," and laughter.) If I were to live until the time he is looking for, when the Church is to be disestablished and disendowed, namely, 100 years hence, I should not be his equal in the use of language. (Hear, hear.) You cannot have equality excepting in the style and manner I have pointed out to you.

The CHAIRMAN : Time.

Mr. SIMPSON : So far we have heard nothing whatever to

give us reason for disestablishing and disendowing the Church. (Cheers.)

Mr. BRADLAUGH : I heard in the last speech one or two words fall from Mr. Simpson which I will hope fell from him in the heat of debate, and on which, therefore, I will make no further comment. I hope I shall not hear them again. These statistics are said only to affect sects. My proposition was that in a State like England, the Church of the majority even ought not to have exclusive privileges, and that the Established Church is not the Church of the majority—(hear, hear)—and I addressed my argument to the question of population. I do not put it in the unde-fined way as to my knowledge in which Mr. Simpson puts it. I stated, as he himself has now affirmed, that there were no reliable statistics on which you could come to an accurate conclusion.

Mr. SIMPSON : Since 1851.

Mr. BRADLAUGH : And as I was dealing with 1876, I spoke of what I meant. (Oh, oh, and cheers.) I could not possibly, in my first speech, deal with anything else than the present time, 1851 had not then been alluded to ; and I ask the noisy Churchman above to make me the same allow-ance now that he did to Mr. Simpson. I stated that, at best, the most that could be claimed by advocates of the Church of England was, that it was the Church of a narrow and decreasing majority, and I then went on to say that, in my opinion, if you took the statistics fairly, it was the Church of an overwhelming minority. Now, Mr. Simpson has dealt with figures. He first says that sects only mean Christian sects. That is not so. (A Voice : "It is so.") You had better buy a lexicon and attend a Definition Bee for a month. (Laughter.) There are Mahomedan sects ; there are Buddhist sects ; and, if you will read Mr. Gladstone's last article in the *Contemporary*, you will find there are sects who do not hold any form of religious creed. (Interrup-tion.) I regret that I had to furnish brains as well as argu-ments to those on the other side. (Cheers) Now, what is the truth ? The truth is that Mr. Simpson's own statistics showed 10,380,661 in 1851 who were not members of the Church of England ; therefore, I was quite right in saying that he was over 5,000,000 out. He says he is only dis-cussing the rights of religious people. Does he mean to say I have no right as a citizen in this State ? Does he mean to say that because, according to his doctrine, there were 4.466,266 non-worshipping people in 1851, and because there are more now, that they have no rights on this question. Why, the proposition is so monstrous that nobody with any sense would accept it. (Cheers.) Then he says that, if the Church of the minority ought not to hold the national property against the will of the majority, the converse would hold good.

Mr. SIMPSON: Public property.

Mr. BRADLAUGH: I say national; and I will prove it. Mr. Simpson has said "public," but he has not told you how the Church got it. I am going to do so before we finish this debate. (Hear, hear, and cheers.) I am quite sure Mr. Simpson will keep clear of that point. I was about to say—and unless he answers my proposition it is nothing at all—I was about to say that the converse of the proposition bears no relation to it—(hear, hear,)—and no one addressing himself logically to the question would so apply it. But if it be true that the Church is in a minority, we need not discuss what the majority may do. (Hear, hear.) On Mr. Simpson's own figures, his own Church was in 1851 in a minority of the population in England alone of 3,233,000,[*] in a minority also in Scotland, and in a minority also in Wales; and he has got to get rid of his own figures before he can say what majority may do at all. (Cheers.) Then, it is not true that the 9th and 10th William III., chapter 32, inflicts the pains and penalties he said it did; it is true that it inflicts the pains and penalties I put. It is not true that they apply to ministers of the Church of England alone. It is not true that in any case the pain and penalty is only being turned out of the Church. I need not enlarge further on that, because I gave an illustration; and I will now address myself to the argument I had sketched out to bring before you. I say that in Wales only a small minority adheres to the Established Church, and, to use the language of the Rev. R. W. Dale, "a national institution which exists for the benefit of a section of the people is a national injustice." Respecting statistics of 1851, it is enough to put on record here that the bishops and archdeacons, in their official charges, admit that the mass of the people are holding aloof from them, and what they call the "tide of Scepticism," is flowing with increasing volume. Now I take you to another

---

* See previous correction.

point of the argument why the Church of England should be disestablished and disendowed. A little while ago the Universities used to be closed to all Dissenters, and even now, to use the words of the Rev. J. G. Rogers, "There are certain offices connected with the Universities which are restricted to clerical members of the Church of England; the headships of colleges, a certain number of fellowships, divinity professorships are all restricted to clergymen of the Church of England. Our contention is that, as these are national seats of learning, this arrangement, in the first place, is an injustice to that portion of the people, whether belonging to the Church or to Dissent, who are shut out from their enjoyment. We say, further, that it is a hindrance to the advance of learning, inasmuch as it diminishes the field for competition; and that it is prejudicial to the advance and free pursuit of truth by giving a certain premium to a man if he will only subscribe to a certain creed, and enter a particular profession, whether he believes the creed and loves the profession or not. On these grounds we do contend that all endowments in the Universities should be perfectly free to all classes of her Majesty's subjects. All that we say is, 'Throw the competition open; let merit win, no matter where that merit is to be found.' (Applause.)" But what was the condition of the Universities when the Church of England had the monopoly of them? And I hardly know what Mr. Simpson considers argument. When I use figures he says it is not a question of figures; when I use facts he says it is not a question of conduct. When the Universities only admitted members of the Church of England, hear how Sir William Hamilton speaks of them—and Sir William Hamilton is not on my side; he is on the side Mr. Simpson represents. He says: "The natural tendency of the academical ordeal was to sear the conscience of the patient to every pious scruple; and the example of "the accursed thing" committed and enforced by ' the priests in the high places, extended its pernicious influence from the Universities throughout the land. England became the country in Europe proverbial for a disregard of oaths, and the English Church in particular was abandoned as its peculiar prey to the cupidity of men allured by its endowments and educated to a contempt of all religious tests." Then he goes on to say: "Oxford is now a national school of perjury" [he is speaking of the time when Dissenters were kept out]. The intrant is made to swear that he will do what he subsequently finds he is not allowed to perform. The candidate for a degree swears that he has done what he has been unable to attempt; and perjures himself by accepting from a perjured congregation an illegal dispensation of performances indispensable by law. The professor swears to lecture as the statutes prescribe, and he does not. The Reverend Heads of Houses, the academical executive, swear to see that the laws remain inviolate, and the laws are violated under their sanction; they swear to be vigilant for the improvement of the University, and in their hands the University is extinguished; they swear to prevent all false oaths, and for their own ends, they deliberately incur the guilt of perjury themselves, and anxiously perpetuate the universal perjury of all under their control." This is the declaration of a man educated in the University. Here is a reason why these places should be thrown open. We were asked: "Are there pains and penalties?" Why do we claim to inter our dead in the churchyards of the Church of England, more than in Jewish or Quaker burial grounds or private cemeteries? Because those churchyards are national property. (Cheers.) Are they national property? Let us see. What is Church property? "Ecclesiastical property is property impressed with a public trust to support such religious services as Parliament from time to time shall appoint." This describes no other property whatever. Lord Coleridge, when Attorney-General, defined Church Endowments as "Endowments given and taken subject to State control, on State terms, upon conditions laid down by the State, and liable to be altered by the power that has laid them down." In fact, and by constitutional usage, Parliament, as part of its current business, does from time to time prescribe the religious uses of the property now dedicated to the Church of England. No man can leave any property to the Church of England to support other uses than what Parliament may prescribe: there is no such thing as the Corporation of the Church of England, which can sue and be sued. The continuous legislation on Church property and directions of Church discipline by Parliament; the relation of State officers with ecclesiastical officers; the redistribution of Church property by the Ecclesiastical Commissioner, and the common law rights possessed by all the inhabitants of a parish, whether they are Churchmen or not—all these flow from the special legal tenure and quality of Church property, viz., that it is property

OF THE ENGLISH CHURCH.

devoted to such religious uses as political authority shall direct. This description applies to no other kind of property whatever. Now, of what does Church property consist? It consists chiefly of monastic lands, tithes, Parliamentary grants, and voluntary endowments. It is not easy to say what is the exact amount of Church property, because the Church has been very careful in keeping its statistics from us. It is estimated by some very much higher than it is estimated by others. A gentleman of the Church of England, the Reverend Mr. Abbott, in 1863, calculated its income at £9,459,565 a year. I have no means of knowing whether that be true or not. If Mr. Simpson knows that it is the right income, I ask him to state it. The Liberation Society calculates the income at about £6,000,000 a year. But I will show you why it is impossible to get at any correct estimate of the income of the Church: a large amount of its property consists of lands habitually under-valued by the Church. There is no doubt about that. I can bring overwhelming instances of under-valuations, if they be denied. In dealing with the valuation of Church property in Ireland, it was found that the clerical valuations and the real valuations differed as far as it was possible for figures to differ. In addition to that, we have the ecclesiastical property in connection with the archbishoprics, the bishoprics, and the cathedrals, the greatest portion of which consisted originally of monastic lands. My opponent says the Church was before the Government was. The Church of England originated in the reign of Henry VIII. (Cries of " No " and " Yes.") Do you say it existed before? (Hear, hear, and disturbance.) Does my opponent say it existed before? Then I will read him such an indictment of the manner in which Church property was obtained before then, from the mouth of a Church of England clergyman, as shall make him wish he had never carried it a bit further. (Cheers.) I will be content to begin with Henry VIII., when he seized the monastic lands, when he stole the property of the Roman Catholic Church—(hear, hear, and groans)—and gave a portion to a number of his pious followers, who were ready to join any religious sect, and the rest of it to the Church, to be used by the Church under Royal supremacy. Several bishoprics and deaneries hold to this day lands so obtained. The value of these is differently stated. Will Mr. Simpson tell us what the value is, so that I may deal with it? The Ecclesiastical Commissioners have to deal with it sometimes. They dealt with some of it under the authority; and I will tell you what they did. They have a lot of poor clergy, to whom they ought to have given it but, amongst other things, they gave the Bishop of Glocester £10,000 to repair his palace; the Bishop of Oxford £46,000; the Bishop of Ripon, £10,000, to build a palace there; and the Bishop of Lincoln, £52,000, to buy an estate there. (A Voice: "Subject.") Subject! This is the subject. (Hear, hear.) I am showing you how your Church authorities are swindling the nation. (Cheers. You wanted Church property, and I am giving it you. The next property is tithes. The Tithes Commutation Act, by which the claim of the tenth of the profits was changed for a rent charge, was passed in 1836, and the last return which I know of—there may be one later, and, if so, I shall be glad to have it from Mr. Simpson—gave the amount of those tithes at £4,050,237. Deducting from those figures the amount taken by the lay tithe-holders, it would leave more than £3,000,000 clear taken by the clergy, without reckoning about £200,000 applied to schools and colleges. How did those tithes originate? According to Sir Robert Phillimore (the Dean of Arches, and the Judge on points of doctrine when the Church and the clergy differ amongst themselves), about the year 794, Offa, King of Mercia, the most potent of all the Saxon Kings of his time, made a law whereby he gave tithes of his kingdom, as a sort of expiation for the death of somebody he had killed. He gave away the property of his people to buy his way into heaven. (Laughter.) And that was extended to the whole of England some years afterwards by Ethelwolf. Now, tithes were of three sorts—prædial tithes, mixed tithes, and personal tithes. The first were tithes of all things springing out of the earth; the mixed tithes were tithes of milk, wool, eggs, pigeons, lambs, pigs, kids, and so on; the personal tithes took part of the individual earnings of the persons from whom the tithe was taken. Now, those tithes were collected in Ireland at the point of the bayonet down to about forty years ago, and they were only commuted in England when, to use the language of Earl Russell, they were such a source of wrangling and ill-will between farmers and clergymen, as to be a positive bar to the cultivation of the land. I shall follow the question of Church property throughout. I say the whole thing, from beginning to end, is iniquitous. I say that the property is national property, and that this Church, which has done nought for the majority whose property it holds, ought to disgorge it for the benefit of the nation. (Cheers.)

Mr. SIMPSON: If my friend, Mr. Bradlaugh, chooses to go to a date previous to this world, I will follow him. (Laughter.) He should not taunt me about going to a certain period in English history for the purpose of keeping me back, probably, or trying to form in my mind some terrible calamity that is likely to befall me. As a disputant Mr. Bradlaugh's duty is this, and I am sorry I should have to point it out; but, before I forget, allow me to say that if I have said anything in my previous speech that was not courteous, or gentlemanly, I apologise to the very core. I will ask Mr. Bradlaugh, at the end of the debate, what it was, and if I can make a more ample apology I am prepared to do so. But Mr. Bradlaugh's duty, as a debater, is to go where he likes, and to see whether I follow him; not to try to frighten me, so that if I do attempt to follow him something disastrous is going to happen to Simpson. (Laughter.) Why the thing is a farce; but it becomes something more than a farce when you listen to him out. He told you at first that he was going to content himself with the history of the Church of England from the time it commenced, and that it was during the time of Henry VIII. "Mind you, it commenced then," said Mr. Bradlaugh. Then what did he go to Ethelwolf for? (Laughter and cheers.) Why go to the year 706, I think, or thereabouts?

Mr. BRADLAUGH: 794.

Mr. SIMPSON: 794, 300 years back of his own estimate when the Church commenced. It is no use, Mr. Bradlaugh, shaking your head; you said it, and to-morrow it will be in print. You are here to-night for the purpose of disestablishing and disendowing the Church, which did not begin until the time of Henry VIII., and yet you have given the history of the tithe transaction that took place in the year 700. I appeal to you, ladies and gentlemen, was there no Church in the year 700 then? (Yes.) If there was no Church, what about the tithes? If there were no tithes, why did you talk about them? But I am anxious, Mr. Bradlaugh, that you should go into the history of the property of the Church, and if you never got flogged in your life I will make you flog yourself. (Cheers.) Mind you, I have not said I will flog him, but I will make him flog himself. We will have nothing but chapter and verse for the history of the Church's property : we will not have the kind of thing he treated us to during the last part of his fifteen minutes. Did you notice it? "No authentic account," said Mr. Bradlaugh, "of the condition of the Church since 1851—none that can be relied upon;" and what did he do immediately afterwards—stepped to the front, stretched himself to his highest—(Shame)—and told you that the Church of England is in a decreasing majority. How does he know it, if there are no statistics to be relied upon? I ask you to think of this. Do not take what I say, ladies and gentlemen. It is for me simply to point out the weak points Mr. Bradlaugh puts forth. When he tells you there is nothing to be depended upon since 1851, then do not you believe what he says when he tells you that the Church is in a decreasing majority, because, from his own account, there are no statistics to be relied upon. (Hear, hear.) He gives us a quotation from somebody whose name I did not happen to catch, as to his opinion of the Church. I will give you one from a gentleman whom I know he respects, and I know that there are thousands, nay, millions, in this country who also respect the same gentleman; and though it was my duty some time ago to do all I possibly could to thwart that gentleman in a certain intention, I, nevertheless, respected the man. I believe him honest and sincere in his convictions, and that what he does he does because he believes it to be for his country's good, and that is the Right Hon. Wm. Ewart Gladstone. (Cheers.) Now, this is the right hon. gentleman's opinion on the question Mr. Bradlaugh is here to sustain, and I wish Mr. Bradlaugh to remark that it is against himself. Mr. Gladstone says that the State, in separating itself from the Church, would entail upon itself a curse; secondly, in doing so, the State would be resisting light and truth, which is the highest sin of man; thirdly, that those who contend that the Church and State ought to be separated, know not the acuteness of Satanic instinct. I will not, like my friend, read you my speech out of a book, but just tell you that that is what Mr. Gladstone says, and the man who has said that—(A Voice: "Forty years ago.") Eh? Mr. Gladstone said it—(A Voice: "When?")—no matter when he said it. Wait till I have finished, if you please. No matter when he said it. (A Voice: "How do you know he did?") If Mr. Gladstone has not repudiated that statement—if he has not recanted it—if you cannot bind him to something that he has said in opposition to that, it does not matter when he said it. I hold Mr Gladstone to it. (Hear, hear, and cheers.) But Mr. Bradlaugh told us that the Church had not done anything to represent the people, or something to that effect—that she had never done anything for the people. Let us see what she has done, and we can speak of this apart from religion, Mr. Bradlaugh, and I think so far we have managed very well. (Hear, hear.) Let us see what she has done for education. Now, I know, Mr. Bradlaugh, that if there is anybody who is anxious for the education of the people of this, and other countries, you are the man—(hear, hear)—and, if I can point you to a sect—to a sect, Mr. Bradlaugh—that has done more for education than it is possible almost for the mind of man to conceive—(Oh, oh, and laughter)—at least give that sect credit for what it has done. That is all I ask. Now, I will tell you what it has done. In 1870—we have got figures for this a little bit later than 1851—in 1870 there were 25.500 schools, 21,000 of which belonged to the Church. (Cheers.) For supporting those schools the Church raises annually £750,000—(hear, hear)—and during the last sixty years she has spent, in maintaining and building schools, £27,000,000. (A Voice : "Public money.") For her missionary work at home and abroad she raises the immense sum of £5.000,000 a year. But Mr. Bradlaugh has told you to-night that the State pays somebody connected with the Church. Will he give us the proof? I am content at present—and he will acknowledge that I am taking the right course—and simply say I want the proof of it. Now, then, I make this affirmation : the State does not pay one single copper to any minister of the Established Church. (Cheers.) Now, then, first, I want Mr. Bradlaugh to prove what he has said. (A Voice : "Who does pay it?") Unless he should fancy I am afraid to follow him, I make the statement ; and, if we are spared till to-morrow night, I will produce the proof. Now, then, touching Church property and national property. Mr. Bradlaugh says that Church property is national property. Then why not be content to say, "The national property used by the Church"? If that is Church property, it is Church property; it cannot be Church property and national property at one and the same time. There is evidently a mistake somewhere. Now, then, I contend that Church property is not, and cannot be, national property.   Let Mr. Bradlaugh give us the evidence to-morrow night that is so terrific and terrible for me to contemplate in the future as to what this Church property really is.   I should only be too glad to follow him ; and, when we have the whole matter out, I am morally certain that you, ladies and gentlemen, will not feel that you have wasted time with us here to-night, because the points we are trying to unravel are points continually set up by the Liberation Society.   I do not include Mr. Bradlaugh in that Society, because he has already repudiated it.   Why he should do so I do not know ; but he has repudiated any connection with it.   (Shame.)

Mr. BRADLAUGH: That is not quite what I said.   On the contrary, what I did say was, that the Liberation Society were not to be held responsible for me.   (Hear, hear.)   Every one will understand why I, Charles Bradlaugh, say that.

Mr. SIMPSON : And I quite understand it, too, and the Liberation Society quite understand it ; but I will not permit the separation—(Oh, oh)—because that which Mr. Bradlaugh advocates here to-night the Liberation Society's orators are advocating throughout the whole of the country night after night.   They are twain in thought on this question ; they are one and one on this question ; and each and all of them are in the exact opposite to that which is true in relation to the Church of England.   (Cheers.)   Well, gentlemen, it is for you to judge.   You have heard Mr. Bradlaugh to-night : has he said anything in favour of disestablishment and disendowment?   (No and Yes.)   No, no ; I will tell you what he has said.   Very probably he is reserving himself for to-morrow night ; and I hope to have the presence of each and all of you ; and then I hope you will mentally come to the conclusion whether it is a political necessity that the Church of England should be disestablished and disendowed.   I beg to move a vote of thanks to the Chairman.

Mr. BRADLAUGH seconded the vote of thanks, which was carried unanimously, and acknowledged by the Chairman.

Mr. BRADLAUGH : With Mr. Simpson's permission, I beg to announce that this discussion is being reported by a reporter engaged by the Joint Committee, and will be published first in the *National Reformer*.   Of course Mr. Simpson will have the right of publishing it anywhere if he pleases.

On the second night the hall was again crowded in every corner, and the excitement was very great; but, on the whole, the audience was very good-tempered.

The CHAIRMAN: Ladies and Gentlemen,—We are about to renew the discussion that was commenced last night. The subject, I believe, you are all now well informed of, and if you will only do as the audience did last night, that is, assist me in keeping order, there can be no doubt that we will have a very pleasant discussion to-night. Both gentlemen who have undertaken the positions they have, seem, I have no doubt, to their friends, to be quite qualified to carry out all that is expected from them. If the friends of Mr. Simpson will show towards the friends of Mr. Bradlaugh the same kind feeling that they did last night, then my business as Chairman will be a sinecure, as it was last night, I am proud to say. A more intelligent meeting I never had the honour of presiding over than the one last night, and I think I may reiterate the same statement to-night. I beg to state distinctly that interruptions to-night will not be allowed for; so that it will be well for each party to keep as quiet as possible. Mr. Bradlaugh has to leave for London by the 11 o'clock train, and we are very desirous indeed to complete this discussion by 10 o'clock. I shall be, as I was last night, as impartial as possible in regard to time. Each gentleman will be called to time, and, no doubt, they will answer the call as they did before. Without any further comment, I now call upon Mr. Bradlaugh to speak for the first half hour. (Cheers.)

Mr. BRADLAUGH: In his last speech last night Mr. Simpson said the State does not pay a single copper to any minister. I will assume that by a copper he means one penny. I thought I had shown uncontradictedly that tithe was a State-ordained payment; and there is surely no moral distinction, and very little technical distinction, between a payment which the State first collects and then pays, and a payment which the State authorises the receiver to collect from those persons upon whom the State imposes the obligation of paying, and, admittedly, on the government return of 1856, more than £3,000,000 of tithes per year do reach the Church; or, instead of a single copper, much more than 720,000,000 coppers. I am not quite sure whether Mr. Simpson disputed the doctrine that the Church of England, as it now exists, was by law established in the reign of Henry VIII.; but, as I think something turns on it, I will take the liberty of proving it to you. And first, I will refer you to Hallam's "Constitutional History of England," in which you will find that, in March 1531, the statute abolishing papal supremacy, and declaring King Henry the supreme head of the Church, was introduced. The statute 26 Henry VIII., chapter 1, is the statute which I say created the Church of England—which I am seeking to disestablish, so far as my argument will do it—making the King the only supreme head of the Church, and giving our Sovereign lord, his heirs and successors, Kings of this realm, full power and authority to change, repress, redress, reform, order, correct, restrain, and amend all such errors, heresies, abuses, contempts, and enormities, whatever they be. Now, somebody asked—and I understood that to seem a feature endorsed by Mr. Simpson—"Can the Queen appoint bishops?" and as this certainly does bear upon the question of the Establishment, it is necessary to refer you to the 25th Henry VIII., where it is directed that a licence from the Crown is to be sent to the Chapter, directing them to choose or elect an archbishop or a bishop. A letter missive is sent with it, nominating the person whom they are to choose, which, if they do not obey or signify the same according to the tenor of the Act within twenty days, they are subject to penalties ; and if the election be not made within twelve days later the King may nominate the bishop by letters patent without any election at all. That clearly disposes of the point as far as it goes. Mr. Simpson asks why, if the present Established Church, according to my doctrine, originated with Henry VIII., I went back to the reign of Ethelwolf? Simply, I answer, because I wanted to trace the origin of the tithe which the Church receives to-day under the Tithe Commutation Act of 1836. Mr. Simpson made no effort to show you that here my facts were wrong, and I may say, without any offence to himself, that none of the propositions which I took considerable care to state last night were in any sort or fashion dealt with by him in his reply. (No, and cheers.) He invented out of his own able and vivid imagination, one or two points that, probably, he thought I ought to have taken, and he replied to those—(laughter)—but he did not reply, as you will see when the report comes to be read, to any one of the series of propositions which went to the root of this question, and with which I opened in my first speech. Mr. Simpson made no effort to show that my facts were wrong: and if my statements were accurate, what then was the worth of his declaration that the Church did not receive a single penny from the State? If the tithes originated as a State payment, by State decree first endorsed by Parliament, afterwards transferred to this Church by the authority of the statute, which I have read to you, which substituted Henry VIII. as supreme head of the Church here, then the whole of the point I have taken is complete. (Hear, hear.) Again, in my statement of Church property taken by the Church from the hands of the State, I included monastic lands. No sort of dispute was, or indeed could be, made as to my correctness on this point, yet every farthing of rental and profit derived from such lands is an effective payment to the Church by the State. Mr. Simpson, in his last speech, amidst great cheering from his supporters, took great credit for the educational work alleged by him to be carried out by the Church, but he forgot that, in my statement of tithes, I had purposely and specially told him that I had not debited the Church with £196,946 per annum of tithes, for I told him that in the £3,000,000 and upwards with which I debited the Church, the amount to laymen, and the amount for educational purposes, were not included according to the House of Commons return of 1856. In stating that not a single copper goes into the hands of any minister of the Church, Mr. Simpson must draw very subtle distinctions between the Church and its ministers, for it is certain that by the Act 58th George III., chapter 45, Parliament voted £1,000,000 of public money for building churches. The Church Building Commission was appointed to spend the money. The Bank of England was authorised to lend it upon Exchequer Bills. The Act did not provide for the repayment of the money, and I have not found that the Church ever did repay it. (Cheers.) In 1824, by the 5th George IV., chapter 103, Parliament voted £500,000 more of State money to the Commissioners, to be disbursed in paying for the building of churches. I need not go through a list of other sums which have been voted from time to time. Lord Althorp carried a resolution in the House of Commons on the 21st April, 1834, that £250,000 should be annually granted for the repair of churches, to be taken from the Land Tax, at this time; that was when there was considerable agitation both here and in Ireland preceding the Tithe Commutation Act. The Church Building Commission extended from 1818 to 1856. Parliament in

1854 passed an Act declaring that it should only last two
years longer. The third report of the Ecclesiastical Commissioners, dated the 18th July, 1856, says that "the funds
entrusted by her Majesty's Government to the Commission
are nearly exhausted." Yet Mr. Simpson says not one
penny comes to the hands of the ministers. If he dis-
tinguishes between the minister and the Church, then the
distinction is one which may serve him technically, but cannot serve him morally, because both are identified together.
(Cheers.) The two commissions were consolidated, but not
until the Church Building Commission had nearly emptied
its coffers of the money voted to it by Parliament, to be spent
in the interests of the Established Church. More than
that, this commission actually provided, as its report shows,
for the way in which the salaries of some of the ministers
were to be raised—namely, by pew rents in the churches,
erected at the expense of the State; and I ask you what
would you say of me if I said to you, "I get nothing from
the State," and you were able to show me that Parliament
had voted money for the shop in which I carry on my
business, for the printing machine with which I print my
paper, and to buy me the paper on which I print it? What
would you say if I said, "I do not get a single penny from the
State," although my business is carried on with State money?
Mr. Simpson refers to the educational work of the Church
of England; but this is extremely unfortunate, because
everyone knows that the Act passed under Mr. Gladstone's
Premiership was rendered necessary because the Church,
which had had up to that time the monopoly of educational
privileges and advantages, had so neglected its work that the
ignorance of the English people in the charge of the Church
had become a byword throughout the world—(Oh, and
cheers)—and, whilst I fully believe that during the last ten
years the Church of England has made desperate efforts to
increase its educational efficiency, yet it is true that at the
present moment the densest ignorance is found in the agricultural and other districts where the Church of England
wields the most local influence. Mr. Simpson said—and I
am sure he would not misrepresent intentionally—that
Messrs. Dale and Rogers had admitted that their tour
through England was a failure. I cannot say whether or
not they have ever said so, but I will tell you what I have
found. In one of his late speeches, Mr. Dale says: "I
have said that Mr. Rogers and I have been addressing a

large number of public meetings in different parts of the country. We are very well satisfied with our work so far as it has gone, and we have received encouragement from the most various sources. We have seen abundant proof that among the rank and file of the Liberal party, and among the local leaders of the Liberal party in those districts of the country we have visited, there is an earnest and resolute purpose to secure, and to secure at an early time, the triumph of our cause." (Loud applause, and cheers.) Therefore, if Mr. Dale said something different at some other time, it is no argument against me ; but as Mr. Simpson thought right to quote to you Mr. Dale's account of his failure from memory, and as his memory deceived him with reference to abstruse calculations of numbers, I thought it might also deceive him on a matter of this kind. (Laughter.) Now, Mr. Simpson, in his last speech, instead of answering any of the matters I had laid before you in favour of disestablishment, read to you some very effective and eloquent words from Mr. Gladstone. I have only one reply to make to that. Against Mr. Gladstone's earlier theories I put Mr. Gladstone's later practices—(hear, hear)—and I answer the eloquent passage, which Mr. Simpson evidently thought better than anything else he could find, with the magnificent precedent of the disestablishment of the Irish Church effected by Mr. W. E. Gladstone. (Cheers.) I say that if the example of one man is to have weight in this debate, then I prefer taking his matured experience, resulting in practice, to his early theories, when he did not understand the subject quite so well as he has done since. (Cheers.) Now Mr. Simpson last night said that, even supposing the Church of England as by law established turned out to be the Church of the minority, that would be no reason for disestablishing or disendowing that Church, as her influence might be so overwhelmingly good as to set all questions of figures on one side. Mr. Simpson did not take the pains to reply to the instances I had given where the influence of the Church was very far from good. On the contrary, he did not pretend that it had been perfect, and said he was not there to defend it from those attacks that I made upon it. In fact, the argument of last night was thus : When there was room for a good joke, with the ability for joking in which I am no equal to Mr. Simpson, the joke was forthcoming ; when it was necessary to answer figures, Mr. Simpson said it was of no conse-

quence, except once, and then I think he wished afterwards
that he had said the same there; and when he came to
facts, then he said they had nothing to do with the question.
Now, first, it is not a question of supposing that the Established Church may be the minority; in point of fact, it is
the Church of the minority.   (Cries of " No," and "Yes.")
On Mr. Simpson's own figures. (No, no, and Yes, yes.)
In 1851 there were in the population of England more than
10,000,000 of people who did not belong to the Established
Church.   Mr. Simpson says that he does not reckon
some 4,400,000 of those, because they did not belong to
any sect at all.   The question is not whether they
belong to a religious body; the question is whether they
are English citizens whose property is taken. (Cheers.)
In 1851, then, on Mr. Simpson's own figures, the Church
was in am inority of nearly 3,000,000 in England.   It was in a
minority of seven-eighths in Wales, and it was in a considerable minority in Scotland.   The minority has grown
smaller since; that is, the majority has increased. (A Voice.
" Prove it.")   Mr. Simpson says, and the eloquent gentleman in the gallery says "Prove it." (Laughter.) I cannot
give you much proof—(Oh, oh)—and I am not at all sure
that the proof I shall offer to you is at all trustworthy
—(Oh, oh)—because it is only the words of the bishops
of the Church. (Cheers.)   I am obliged to be extremely
careful, because I have the authority of the *Courier* for
saying that I got out of temper last night, and I am afraid
I am likely to do the same thing to-night. (Laughter.) The
bishops, commencing with the Bishop of Ripon, in his triennial
charge, printed in the *Leeds Mercury*, delivered only a few
weeks ago, laments the increase of the number of people
who do not attend the Church; and I will undertake to say
that out of the whole of the visitation charges of the bishops
and archdeacons, you will not find me ten per cent. during
the last five years that have not repeatedly lamented the increase of people who do not go to church. This has been so
much so that they have actually held conferences in London
and in other parts of the country, to see how they could
get them there, which they clearly would not do if they were
crowding in.   So that, on the statements of the clergy themselves, it may be taken that the minority which existed in
1851 is at least as large; that is, that the majority against
it has not decreased, but the minority sum is represented
by a less figure than it was twenty years ago. Now, leaving

the question of minority, we will come to the question of her influence for good. What is her influence for good in the matter of burials? (A Voice: "Better than yours; what would you do?" and laughter.) How does her influence for good act on the Burial Question? And I will say, for the benefit of the gentleman who has interrupted me this moment, that I have no influence on the Burial Question, or I would bury him at once. (Laughter.) Mr. John Bright, in Parliament, last year, said: "It is admitted that the parochial burial ground is intended for the service of all the inhabitants of the parish; that all have a right to use it when their friends come to be buried. Generally, the parochial burial ground has been created and maintained at the expense of the parish. At any rate, up to the time of the abolition of Church rates, the burial grounds were provided and supported by the parish. I assume," says Mr. Bright, "that all the burial grounds that were in existence before the passing of the Church Rates Abolition Act, were established at the cost of the parish; and, therefore, now are—as indeed they all are by law—the property of the parish.' I am confining myself to the Church of England burial grounds. Now, there are 13,000 parishes in England where there are no burial conveniences, except those of the Established Church; and Mr. Simpson asked last night whether there were any pains and penalties, and said there were no pains and penalties. I gave you pains and penalties, political and social, inflictable under the Act of Parliament. But are there no pains and penalties to the families and relatives of unbaptised dead? (Hear, hear; and a Voice: "What an idea!") A gentleman says "What an idea!" Why, is it not true that the Church of England has refused, because a little child eight days old has not been baptised, although the clergyman has been asked to baptise it—is it not true that the Church of England has refused it the rite of burial, and has had it taken at night for burial like a dog? (Hear, hear, and Shame!) In a pamphlet published by J. Carvell Williams, which you may read with great advantage, you will find a case stated in which, in West Retford, the vicar having been asked to baptise a child who was ill, promised to come, and did not: the child died; and then the vicar told the father that he would not read the service over it, and that if they wished the child buried in the churchyard, they must bring it after dark. (Shame!) Now, Sir, is not this a pain and a penalty to the mother and the father? Is not this a pain and a penalty to the weeping children? (A Voice: "The subject.") It is the subject. We intend to take these graveyards out of the hands of the Church of England, by the disestablishment of the Church. (Loud cheers.) Mr. May, a Wesleyan, of Sutton-Court Farm, applied to the rector of Little Mongeham, where there is a churchyard, but no church, for permission to bury his child. The child had not been baptised, and the vicar——I am bound to say in this instance most courteously——stated that he was, by law, prohibited from reading the service over the child, and that they must bring it after dark, and bury it without service. In Ashby Hall, another case of the same kind occurred, where the vicar first consented, and then went away and left his curate, who refused to bury it. When the parents complained to the rector he stated that, if he had clearly understood that the child had not been baptised, he should not have consented to the funeral. In point of fact, let the Church of England clergyman be ever so kind, the law prohibits him from burying an unbaptised person. Is not this a pain and penalty? (Hear, hear.) According to Mr. Simpson's own statement, there are 4,400,000 people non-worshippers. Are these 4,400,000 people to be left without the rights of decent burial. We cannot help it. We have to pay, and we claim the right; and we will break up your Church if it does not give it to us. (Cheers.) I find I am approaching the end of my time. I will, therefore, not open out now any new matter; but I will draw your attention to the fact that the whole case opened by me yesterday evening has not been touched. I stated logically and legally the position of the Church, and showed where it got its income from. I did not deny that a portion of it might come from voluntary endowment. (A Voice: "Question!") The question is, "Is the Disestablishment and Disendowment of the Church of England a Political Necessity?"——(No, Yes, and cheers)——and I say that a Church which is only a Church of a minority of the people; a Church which is fat whilst the people are lean; a Church which has rich bishops who do not do their duty by the poor; a Church which has an enormous income; a Church which builds palaces whilst the labourers are starving, is a Church which ought to be disestablished. (Loud cheers.)

Mr. SIMPSON: It is very gratifying to me to have earned such a compliment from Mr. Bradlaugh as that which I have heard this evening. I did not anticipate that he would, before he left Liverpool, admit that in one line of business I was his master. I hope, before I have finished, to con‑vince him, whether he admit it or not, that I am his master in more ways than that of being a joker, because it is my intention to stick closely to the question we have called you together to hear us discuss. Mr. Bradlaugh may wander over a thousand and one questions if he likes ; he may speak the most pleasant thoughts ; give birth to most brilliant sentences and ideas ; display the ability natural to himself, well-cultivated as a rhetorical speaker : but all that will not influence or move me from this fact—that I accepted his challenge to discuss a certain question, and that question only will I discuss. (Cheers.) I ask Mr. Bradlaugh what has the Burials Bill to do with the question ? (Hear, hear.) I ask Mr. Bradlaugh, supposing he stood in my shoes in this discussion, and I stood in his in the same discussion, could he not now say to me, as I say to him, "You have introduced a topic which does not demonstrate the desira‑bility or necessity of disestablishing and disendowing the Church of England"? (Oh, and cheers.) I will tell you why I say so. I am here to-night to say, in opposition to Mr. Bradlaugh, that the disestablishing and disendowing of the Church of England is not a political necessity—(hear, hear) —and yet, ladies and gentlemen, it is known, I think, to almost every one within these walls, that whatever power and ability I possess, I have used it in favour of obtaining for Dissenters unlimited license, along with others, for burial in Church of England churchyards. (Cheers.) Why, sir, we can have all that Mr. Bradlaugh asked for in his last speech on this question of burial, and we can have it with‑out either disestablishing or disendowing. (Cheers.) If we can have it, as he says we are going to have it, if we can have all this without disestablishing and without disendow‑ing, then I submit to you as a logician—(laughter)—well, then, I submit to you as logicians—(laughter and cheers) —that it is not a necessity to disestablish and disendow before you can obtain for Dissenters that which Mr. Brad‑laugh claims for them on the burial question. Now, then, I need say no more on that, because that is disposed of. (Laughter.) Mr. Bradlaugh says I did not answer his facts. Well, I should be a very great simpleton to dispute a fact. Mr. Bradlaugh does not suppose for one moment that I am so far gone as to dispute facts. (Laughter.) When Mr.

Bradlaugh did me the honour—and I consider it an honour, ladies and gentlemen—when he did me the honour to challenge me, and accepted me on my own personality, I cannot for one single moment suppose that he thought he was going to deal with a fool. (Hear, hear.) Then, if he thought he was not going to deal with a fool—(A Voice: "Question.") It is no use your crying out question. I am bound to follow Mr. Bradlaugh in everything he says. Mr. Bradlaugh complains that I have not answered his facts. I admitted his facts, whatever they were. I did not attempt to answer them. (Oh, and laughter.) But, ladies and gentlemen, he uttered not one single fact in favour of the proposition he was here last night to defend—(cheers)—and that I will leave to your unbiassed judgment, when you come to read the verbatim report. (Hear, hear.) Now, then, what says Mr. Bradlaugh, speaking of my remark last night that the Church of England did not receive one single copper? He tries to upset all that is contained in the language of mine by a statement—I have not taken it exactly down, but I think it was that the Church of England has received from the State the sum of £1,500,000.

Mr. BRADLAUGH : Oh, more than that.

Mr. SIMPSON : Well, £2,000,000.

Mr. BRADLAUGH : More than that.

Mr. SIMPSON : Well, £2,500,000. Ladies and gentlemen, I submit that the figures given by Mr. Bradlaugh to you as two sums in payment were two separate and distinct sums—one of £2,000,000 and some odd thousands, and the other of £1,500,000 and some odd thousands ; and he says because the Church has received these sums of money, which he has named, they are State payments, in contradiction to the position I took last night. Now, what was my statement last night ? That the Church did not receive a copper. I meant by that that the ministers of the Church did not receive anything from the State in the form of salaries. (Oh, oh.) I meant by that, they did not now ; and understand me, ladies and gentlemen, will you please, we are here in 1876, I think, and we are discussing the question of the desirability—nay, the necessity—of disendowing and disestablishing the Church of England in 1876. (Hear, hear.) We are not discussing the necessity of disendowing and disestablishing her in the year 700—(cheers) nor any other date between that date and now, but it is the necessity of doing it now—(hear, hear)—and my language had distinct and unmistakeable reference to the present and not to the past. Now then, ladies and gentlemen, a little further on this matter. I at once admit that the Church has received money from the State; and I will do more than Mr. Bradlaugh has done—I will assist him to-night as I did last night. (Laughter.) I will give him the exact figures. You must be a little bit patient, because, when I have to reply to a gentleman, not knowing what he is going to say, I cannot put my hand immediately on the page I want. Before I give you these figures I want you to notice the argument advanced by Mr. Bradlaugh—that because the Church of England had received at a certain period a certain sum of money which he named, *ergo*, the Church was State paid. Now, then, this is the sum which the Church has received. And, by the way, the Church of England is not the only Church which has received money. (Cheers.) Will Mr. Bradlaugh contend to-night that every Church which has received money from the State is a State-paid Church? (Hear, hear.) Will he contend that, by virtue of being a so-called State Church, it ought to be disestablished and disendowed? If he will, all I can say is, let what I am about to read to you speak for itself, and let us see how many Churches we would have left. (Hear, hear.) As Mr. Bradlaugh is very anxious, equally with myself, to have authority for everything which is said, particularly when it is from a book. I tell him that if he will refer to the *Leed's Money* he will find that it gives a Parliamentary return of public money supplied for instruction or religious worship throughout the kingdom: "Church of England, £2,600,000; Church of Ireland, £1,749,818; Church of Rome, £365,607—(shame)—Church of Scotland, £522,182; Protestant Dissenters—of whom Mr. Bradlaugh is on this occasion a most intellectual champion—Protestant Dissenters that are not State paid, bear in mind—"£1,019,547." (Cheers.) Now, that is not all. The Church of England also receives, at a lower period, a further sum of money amounting to £4,441 3s. 2d—you see how careful we Church people are; we give it you in coppers—making a total that the Church of England has received from the State of £2,604,441 3s. 2d. Now, then, ladies and gentlemen, after this honest admission of mine, Mr. Bradlaugh, I hope, will be perfectly satisfied, at least that I am prepared to follow him in his facts, because I give you figures in excess of those he has stated. And yet, ladies and gentlemen, my position of last night is not disturbed. (Laughter.) Now, if you think that it is disturbed, note the argument—that the Church of Scotland is a State-paid Church, Dissenters are State-paid Chapels, the Church of Rome is a State-paid Church, and every institution, every sect that has received money from the State, by virtue of Mr. Bradlaugh's position, is a State-paid Church. (Hear, hear.) Gentlemen, that is not so, and I will tell you why. Because the moneys I have quoted to you—and Mr. Bradlaugh's amount is entered in those I have quoted—are moneys given by the State for certain special and specific purposes. (Hear, hear.) But I contend—and we have no word to the contrary to be relied upon, at any rate, so as to affect our judgment on the question under consideration—that my statement of last night remains untouched. But Mr. Bradlaugh does try to touch it. I admit he tries. (Laughter.) He says in substance, what is the difference between tithes paid into the State coffers and by the State paid back to the Church, and money paid after some other fashion? Why, the difference is this, ladies and gentlemen, that the tithes belong absolutely to the Church, and the State has nothing whatever to do with them—(cheers)—except—(Oh, and laughter)—well, you know, you burst out and laugh before I have finished my sentence—except to do towards that property as the State does towards all and every other property—throw legal protection around it, and see that it is properly disbursed. (Cheers.) Do you build a Dissenting chapel? Do you build a Roman Catholic place of worship? Do you build a Presbyterian chapel? Does some kind, good, and pious man, or men, build and endow these places? (A Voice : " Brewers.") Do they die and do they leave them in trust for ever, to be conducted after a certain form of worship? (Hear, hear.) What does the State do in that case? It protects the wishes of the dead man. (Cheers.) Do you slave and toil here in Liverpool, commercially and otherwise, to obtain a little wealth for those you leave behind? Do you leave a will stating how you desire that money to be laid out or used in the future? What does the State do for you? It takes care that after you are dead, your living behests are carried out to the full letter. (Cheers.) I say—and I say it without the slightest fear of honest, argumentative, rational contradiction—that the Church does not receive one single copper from the State—(hear, hear, and cheers)—that a revenue amounting,

I must again instruct my friend, Mr. Bradlaugh, to a sum of £4,200,000 annually, is raised from tithes, donations, and sundry other ways and means, left by good and pious people for the special purpose. (Cheers.) And the State does no more towards the Church than it does towards any other bequest : it takes care that it is properly carried out. Now, then, one step further on this. The tithe-rent charge, or rental, or revenue, derived by the Church at the present time amounts to the sum of £2,000,000 as money receivable from tithes before the Reformation. £2,200,000 is the sum of money received by the Church, not from tithes, but from money absolutely invested on her behalf by persons who have lived and died since the Reformation. Why, Sir, in the diocese of Manchester only, within the life of the last and the present bishops, we have had built 150 churches, and these churches have been endowed by good and pious men. (Cheers.) That endowment will last as long as England lasts, I hope—(cheers)—and the law that I trust will protect my living wish when I am dead will, I hope and trust, protect the wishes of those who, in their desire to do their country and their countrymen service, have given of their wealth to the benefit of God. (Cheers.) But, ladies and gentlemen, I am not here for the purpose of discussing the question of tithes. I have been led—because Mr. Bradlaugh is bound to lead me if he can—away from the subject. (Cheers.) And not only that, but he is bound to lead you. (Laughter.) Now, then, I must bring you back again, and tell you that he spoke away from the subject when he entered upon it, and I have spoken away from the subject when I followed him ; but I have done it, ladies and gentlemen, because he has given me nothing on the question to grapple with. (Cheers.) Now, then, Mr. Bradlaugh brings a charge against the Church, and that charge is in opposition to a statement that I made last night. Now, how it is in opposition I am at a loss to understand. I simply quoted figures showing what I thought—as I believed that Mr. Bradlaugh was in favour at least of education—that he would be delighted to know, namely, that the Church had done more for education than all the other sects put together—(cheers)—and I thought that, however much he might want to destroy her for other general reasons, he would, at least, respect her for that one act of good. (Cheers.) I quoted the following figures. I think it was 24,000 schools that existed at the last census, and 21,000 of these were Church of England schools, only 3,000 of them belonging to Dissenting bodies. (Cheers.) Now, ladies and gentlemen, if it is a charge against the Church, that she has neglected the poor, that she has neglected the ignorant, and yet she has built 21,000 schools, how does the charge lie against those people whom Mr. Bradlaugh represents, who have only built 3,000 schools? (Cheers.) Let us disestablish and disendow the whole lot. (Hear, hear.) Mr. Bradlaugh wished you to believe, and he tried to convince you in his able roundabout manner —(laughter)—that the Queen did create bishops. Now, ladies and gentlemen, my time is almost up, and I cannot follow any gentleman through the points he may raise in the course of half an hour, but I must tell you it is not in harmony with the facts of the case. The truth is that a bishop is ordained, and is ordained by the people of his own Church, and he receives his appointment only from the Crown. Now that is the difference. Mr. Bradlaugh said it was that the figures I quoted last night showed a loss of memory. Now, I will touch upon this to show you how carefully Mr. Bradlaugh must be watched in this discussion. Ladies and gentlemen, I appeal to you who were here last night, how could it be a loss of memory when I took up a book and read from it, and I passed the book over to Mr. Bradlaugh, and he read from the same book? (Cheers.) There was no loss of memory. The difference between us was this, that I dealt faithfully, truthfully, and honestly with the question we are here to discuss. I took the Church of England as a sect numbering seven millions of souls, and I stated from the return I held in my hand that she outnumbered by two millions every other sect in this country. (Cheers.) Very well, I gave the figures out here in this hall, you made your own calculations—was I right or was I wrong? (Cries of " Right " and " Wrong.") Mr. Bradlaugh did this, and bear in mind he did this after we told him that he knew nothing at all about the question when he opened it—he added four millions of persons to it that were put down in the return as not belonging to any sect. Now, ladies and gentlemen, my challenge was—and I challenge Mr. Bradlaugh to-day, and will prove it, and stand by the report —my challenge was, that the Church of England was two millions in excess of any other sect. (Cheers.) As we were speaking of a religious sect when I spoke of the Church of England—(No, Yes, Hear, hear, and cheers). Well, was I speaking of an irreligious sect? (No.) I contend that my language was only fairly open to the construction that "other sects" meant other religious sects. (Hear, hear.)

Mr. BRADLAUGH: On the mere question of figures, the proposition affirmed by me in my first speech was, that in a State like England, the Church of the majority even ought not to have exclusive privileges, and that the Established Church is not the Church of the majority; and it could be no argument against me to omit 4,400,000 people, and then say you were calculating the minority and the majority fairly. Mr. Simpson is very kind, and I dare say he will oblige me with those figures from the *Leeds Mercury* which he used. (Hear, hear.) Now, if you please, we will just see—because it is a very fair challenge as Mr. Simpson has put it—whether it is true, yes or no, that the Church is in receipt to-day of any money from the State. Mr. Simpson said that he admitted my facts of last night. Well, but amongst those facts I read the last Parliamentary return, showing that the total amount of tithes in 1856—rent charge in lieu of tithes—was £4,050,237, of which I said about £3,000,000 I debited to the Church, not including in that the amount put down for educational purposes. But that amount is also receivable to-day. Mr. Simpson says before the Reformation. It only leaves £2,200,000 of tithes which were enjoyed prior to the Reformation. He has not been good enough to show me that the return, which he says he admitted, was wrong. Either he was wrong in what he put in his last speech, or he was wrong before. Either he is wrong in admitting my facts, or he is wrong in contradicting them—I do not know which. (Laughter.) Now, he is good enough to tell you very properly that the money voted to Protestant Dissenters was voted for specific purposes.

Mr. SIMPSON: The whole of the money.

Mr. BRADLAUGH: The whole of the money for specific purposes. Will he be kind enough to find for me amongst those specific purposes the amount of money voted for building Dissenting Chapels? (Cheers.) Because I read to him £1,500,000 voted in 1818 and 1824 for building churches, and I read to him after that an annual allowance, continued for some years after 1824, of £250,000 for building churches. Your figures are wrong somewhere, Mr. Simpson. (Laughter.) You have been good enough to say you admitted my facts. I was obliged to you, because

I knew you would not dispute anything which was correct. (Laughter.) But, as these were all for specific purposes, would you mind telling me whether Parliament has voted the sums of money you refer to for the same kind of specific purposes that I have just read to you? I admit that there have been aids of various kinds—(Oh!)—I have never denied it. (Cheers.) If I had been in Parliament I should have voted against every one of them. (Laughter.) But that is not quite the question. (Hear, hear.) When Mr. Simpson shows you that the same kind of support— because now he has put it on that basis—is given to the Church of Rome—we may leave out the Church of Ireland, because that has been disestablished—and to the Church of Scotland, and to the Dissenting bodies right through, as is given to the Church of England, then there would be something in it. " But," says Mr. Simpson, " the truth is that the Church has received no such money as Mr. Bradlaugh says at all, because the tithes are not property that the Parliament has anything whatever to do with, except as it has to do with all property, putting a legal protection round it." If that be true, why did Parliament, in 1836, cancel the right of the clergy to collect personal, prædial, and mixed tithes, and establish rent charges in lieu of them? (Cheers.) I am not aware that Parliament does that with general property. Besides, was I right in giving you an account of the origin of tithes last night? That is admitted. Mr. Simpson says he admitted my facts. But was King Offa the pious ancestor who gave away what did not belong to him? Was King Ethelwolf the pious ancestor who gave away what did not belong to him? Was King Athelstan the pious ancestor who gave away what did not belong to him? (Proof.) But the proof is admitted. Your own champion has admitted it. (Cheers.) In a frank and very courteous manner, knowing the effect of that, Mr. Simpson says, " I admit the facts." He says he was not fool enough to dispute them. Well, the last thing I should suspect Mr. Simpson of being would be of being a fool. I admit he is the wisest champion the Church could have here—(laughter)—and he frankly said he did not deny my facts. Well, but if he did not deny my facts, why is it then that he did not reckon the annual value of the land which I showed was taken away from the monasteries and abbeys by Henry VIII., and a portion of which, at any rate, forms part of the Church lands down to this very day? Mr. Simpson says that pious people left these tithes; but the whole of the law is against him. There is evidence of the statutes under which they were collected; there is no evidence of pious people leaving them. (Oh!) And I would ask him how could any pious person ever have left to the Rev. Francis Lundy, rector of Lockington, in the East Riding of Yorkshire, the right in 1832 to summon Jeremiah Dodworth for 4s. 4d., being the tithe of his personal earnings? (Cheers.) The pious man who left Jeremiah Dodworth's earnings to the Rev. Francis Lundy must have been a pious rogue. (Laughter.) I admire Mr. Simpson's notion of piety very much, but what would Jeremiah Dodworth think about it? (Laughter.) Jeremiah Dodworth refused to pay. This was in 1832. A warrant of distress was issued against Jeremiah Dodworth's goods and chattels, and, there not being enough to satisfy the distraint warrant, he was sent to Beverley Castle for three months, working out his punishment for not paying what Mr. Simpson says a pious man left to the Church. (Laughter.) Could any pious man leave a tithe of the growing crops, a tithe of the little sucking pigs, a tithe of the lambs, a tithe of the milk, a tithe of the butter? Why, the figures have got into your head, Mr. Simpson, and the pious ancestor has evolved from the confusion. (Laughter.) Now, Mr. Simpson says: "What has the Burials Bill to do with the disestablishment of the English Church?" Mr. Simpson especially urged last night that there were no pains and penalties on any class of citizens, and it was a fair argument for me to bring that *per contra*, to show that there were. (Hear, hear.) Again he says: "You can get into the burial ground without disestablishing." That is true, but it is also true that, at present, the bench of bishops and the majority of the Established clergy will not let us, and it is only the threat of disestablishment which may bring them up to their bearings on this question. (Cheers, and a Voice: "You want the money, do you?") I should like very much to get it. (Laughter.) I have no belief myself in the blessings of poverty, so I will not pretend to have. (Renewed laughter.) Mr. Simpson asks: "What has the Burials Bill to do with this question?" Why, this—that the churchyards of the Church of England, as I explained in my speech last night, are in a different position to Jewish burial grounds or Quaker burial grounds, or Dissenting burial grounds, which are the property of the particular sect ; they are national property. (No.) Show me the pious man who left them. (Laughter and cheers.) Why, the witch of Endor could not raise his ghost if she tried. (Laughter.) Well, now, Mr. Simpson says that the Crown does not appoint the bishops of the Church. He says the bishops are ordained by their own Church, and then goes on to say, "but they are appointed by the Crown." Yes, but the question is : Can the Church ordain as bishop any body the Crown does not appoint? (A Voice : "Yes.") You say "Yes;" but the Act of Parliament which I read— and Mr. Simpson admitted my facts—the Act of Parliament which I read says that, in the event of the parties not appointing the one named in the letter missive, the Crown can proceed to nominate without their election at all. Is not that as conclusive as any language can be? "Oh, but," says Mr. Simpson, "the Church is in the same position as any other body. Good people build chapels and leave them, and the law protects them." But the difference is, that these chapels have not got an income of more than £3,000,000 a year of tithes. They have not got 13,000 parishes with graveyards belonging to the people. They have not got lands that have been in the hands of the Church ever since Henry VIII. stole them from the Church of Rome. (Cheers.)

Mr. SIMPSON : In no way have I, throughout the two nights' discussion we have had, uttered one single sentence that was calculated by the nature of that sentence to awaken any emotion excepting that of an intellectual character in your breast. I have not talked about plunder ; I have not talked about stealing ; I have not talked about anything excepting that which I have been obliged to talk about, to show you that my friend, Mr. Bradlaugh, knows nothing whatever about the question we are discussing—(cheers)— and, not only that, but to do, as I said I would do to-night —make him flog himself. (Oh.) He says I admit his facts. Gentlemen, so I do; but I do not admit that all that he says is a fact. (Cheers.) There is a difference there, is not there? I tell you that he has not given one single fact in the whole of this discussion—(Oh, oh)—as touching, understand me, the question we have been called together to discuss. That he has given facts in relation to matters and things having no part in connection with the question under consideration I admit, but on the question we are met here to discuss not one single fact has he given. He says I admitted his facts about tithes. He gave us none. (Oh, cheers and groans.) Perhaps, ladies and gentlemen, as you have so kindly allowed Mr. Bradlaugh to do more with books than with his own intellectual power, on this occasion you will allow me to do a little with books, and I will give you authorities which—I care not whether you are Dissenters, Roman Catholics, or Churchmen—I think you will say are at least higher, much higher, than either Mr. Bradlaugh or Mr. Simpson. I will give you the authority of Blackstone, Selden, Southey, Horace Mann, a Dissenter, Lord Selborne, Lord Eldon, and lastly, Lord Brougham. These gentlemen declare—I cannot stop, ladies and gentlemen, to give you their quotations in full, because I have only fifteen minutes, but I can tell you this, and I have never deceived a Liverpool audience in my life —these gentlemen all declare that the Church of England has a perfect and undisputed right and claim to what are called tithes. (No, and cheers.) Ladies and gentlemen, I tell you it is true. Well, then, hear the quotations. It is better for me to deal with one part, and finish it off properly, than ramble off to another. But, by the way, the Liberation Society itself admits that position which I am taking. The Liberation Society says, in the Anti-State Church Tract, page 78—I have not got it with me, Mr. Bradlaugh; I will give you all I can, the quotation and the page. I have done more for Mr. Bradlaugh than he has for me, for I passed him the books, and he never passed one of his yet. (Cheers.) The Liberation Society says: "Such free gifts were much augmented in course of time, since it can be proved from documentary evidence that in the third century" —and, mind you, this is from Nonconformist sources. Mr. Bradlaugh last night was only in the seventh century, but here we have tithes in the third century admitted, and admitted by the Liberation Society itself. (Cheers.) I cannot stop to give you the quotations, for I have only fifteen minutes to speak in—(Go on)—but I tell you that Blackstone, Selden, Southey, Horace Mann, Lord Selborne, Lord Eldon, and Lord Brougham all confirm this, that the tithes from which the Church derives so large a revenue— (a Voice: "What Church?")—the Church of England I am talking about—have belonged to her, and we have direct proof of it, down as far as the third century. And where I can show you and intelligent people that a Church or a system has been in the receipt of certain moneys from certain sources from the third century up to the present time, I ask you, do not I make out a good case of ownership—(cheers)—and do not I show you at the same time that the State pays nothing towards the Church? (No, and cheers.) Now, then, gentlemen, there are taxpayers here. (Oh!) Oh, I know that, and I know that there are taxpayers here who pay some attention to the Chancellor's Budget when it comes out year after year. You criticise it, and you examine the figures with care and caution, and you look to find out. (Hear, hear). Now, I ask you, is there a single man or woman within these walls—do you know of a single man or woman without these walls—(a Voice: " Lots," and laughter)—who has ever found in the Chancellor's Budget one single copper as money to be paid, chargeable against the people of this country, and for which you are to be taxed? (Hear, hear, and cheers.) Of the £78,000,000 taken from us there is not one copper put down for paying the Church clergy; and yet we have Mr. Bradlaugh coming here and saying that the clergy are State-paid. (Cheers.) As another proof that the State does not recognise tithes as a thing within herself, I ask you this question, Can you find on the document I have referred to, that is, our national annual financial statement, either credit or debit for the amount of tithes received by the Church? Certainly not. It is neither credited nor debited. Why? Because it is not by the State received —(cheers)—and if it is not by the State received, how in heaven's name can it be by the State paid? (Cheers.) If it is not by the State paid, and yet it is paid, who pays it? (A Voice: "Simpson," and laughter.) Well, you are quite right; that is, you are right in part. I do pay part, for I have a piece of property that has a tithe on it. And I pay it with pleasure; and I will tell you why, because if I did not pay that tithe to the Church I should have to pay it to the landlord. The land would be worth more to the landlord than it is at present, and I should have to pay him; and I prefer paying it to the Church. (Cheers.) That is exactly the whole gist of this question. The tithe rent is simply a charge left upon the land that certain persons have to pay in the form of a little rent, which they would have to pay as a landlord's rent if they had not to pay it as a tithe rent. Mr. Bradlaugh has given us a fact—oh yes, and it is a cogent fact, too—for disestablishing and disendowing. He told us that the Dissenting bodies were not in receipt of £4,200,000 a year, and as they were not in receipt of that amount of money, the Church ought to have it taken away from her, and the Dissenters ought to have it divided amongst them. (Laughter and cheers; and a voice: " No.") You can come to no other conclusion when a gentleman states here that one Church is rich and another is poor; and he would disestablish and disendow as a matter of necessity. (Question.) That is the question. I contend that, when he gives us these two statements, the common sense argument to be drawn from them is, that he would enrich one at the cost of the other. (No, and Yes.) I reiterate that, so far as this discussion has gone, Mr. Bradlaugh has not kept to the question upon which I was challenged. I have done the best I could to follow him step by step, and because I have been kind to him in following him—(Oh)— because I have been kind to him in lending him my books; because I have been kind to him in telling him I admit his facts, he takes it for granted that I am foolish enough to accept everything he says as a fact. Ladies and gentlemen, that he believes it to be true, I believe. I give him credit for the same amount of honesty and sincerity on this question that I claim and ask you to accord to myself.

Mr. BRADLAUGH: Whilst I give Mr. Simpson credit for thorough sincerity, I must at the same time debit him with a very bad memory, because he says that he thinks I wish to take the £4,200,000, which he admits the Church gets, from the Church of England, and give it to the Dissenting bodies, although he heard me distinctly say that, if I were in Parliament, I should vote against any State payment to any religious body—(cheers)—so that, giving him credit for sincerity, I am obliged to debit him with a bad memory. (Laughter.) He says that my facts he admits, so far as they are facts. Why did he not draw attention specially to those that were not. (Hear, hear.) He says that I did not give you a single fact about tithes. How is it, then, that he complained of my taking you back to the time of Ethelwolf? How is it he did not go into my tracing the tithe property, as I did last night with considerable care, as the report will show you when it is printed? Then, I do not know what Mr. Simpson means by saying that I was in the seventh century last night. If he means the era of Ethelwolf, that is not the seventh. If he means the era of Offa, that is not the seventh. One is the eighth and the other the ninth. It is not of very much importance, but, as Mr.

Simpson thought it worth while to reproach me with it, he might as well have been correct. (Hear, hear.) Then Mr. Simpson quotes to you the names of Blackstone, Selden, Brougham, and a number of others, for the doctrine that the Church has a perfect and undisputed right and claim to tithes. So it has under the statutes—(hear, hear)—but in no other way. (Cheers.) If Mr. Simpson meant that Blackstone traces tithes back to the third century, he does not. I cannot charge my memory with what Selden and Brougham say about it, and Mr. Simpson has not given it me; but I know that Blackstone does not, and I do not think that anybody who will carefully argue it will say that they do, because England was not, in the third century, one undivided and complete Government right through; and it is, therefore, folly of the worst kind to talk of the Church being in uninterrupted receipt of tithes from the third century to the present time. Again, it is quite clear that no pious man can have given tithes of a person's labour then unborn. (Hear, hear.) Mr. Simpson did not touch that at all, but carefully avoided it. Well, then, he says, " Do you find anything in the Budget for paying the clergy?" No, you do not. (Hear, hear.) Neither do you find in the Budget the local poor rates. Neither do you find in the Budget many matters levied upon you by authority of particular statutes. (A Voice: " Chaplains' salaries.") But if we had a Budget made out, showing the burdens cast upon the country by statute, then the Budget would contain the rent charge created in lieu of tithes by the Act of Parliament of 1836, and would also contain the annual value of the lands dedicated to the Reformed Church under Henry. Mr. Simpson says, because it is neither credited nor debited in the Budget, the State does not pay it. If this is only a form of words, it is a bad form—a very bad form. It is so nearly inaccurate that I cannot distinguish between it and it not being true. (Laughter.) Mr. Simpson has put himself in evidence in this case. He says that he has a piece of land on which he pays tithes. Why does he pay rent charge in lieu of tithe on that land? Because there is an Act of Parliament, passed in 1836, which says he shall, and which gives the means of recovering it if he does not, and that is the only means of recovering it. (Cheers.) Mr. Simpson says that in this debate nothing has been raised by me as a ground for the disestablishment of the Church. On the contrary, I have made out a case, first on logical propositions, next followed by facts, which it has not been attempted to deal with in any way. I have contended, and I do contend, that the Church of the minority has no right to take even the admitted £4,200,000—and I say that the amount is much larger, for I say that the lands which I drew your attention to, if properly valued, would show a much larger income than this. I say that when Mr. Simpson tells you about pious people who left tithes to the Church, he should offer some evidence of these things, especially when I have quoted the statute of the realm against him. It is not a fair way of meeting a debate of this kind. Now, why ought the Church of England to be disestablished? Because, at the present moment, it is the cause of division and strife right through the country. (Hear, hear, No, and cheers.) Why, the result of its education and its good spirit was manifested in this very hall with rotten eggs sent against Nonconformist advocates on this platform! It shows how badly the Church has educated those of whom she has had the charge. (Cheers and groans.) I say that the Church is illiberal, and I say that its illiberality is shown by its illiberal conduct. The Bishop of Lincoln would not even allow a Wesleyan minister to record on a tombstone a simple description of his calling. The pains and penalties I dealt with last night have not been answered. What might this Church have been? It might have been the leader of progress in this country. (Hear, hear.) It has been for aristocracy against the people; it has been for tyranny against law. (Hear, hear, and groans.) There are exceptionally liberal men in the Church of England, like Dean Stanley; but how do the bulk of the clergy treat such men? There are men who struggle for the agricultural classes, like Canon Girdlestone; but how does the Church treat them? What is the reason for the disestablishment of this Church? I will tell you. Its Bishops in the House of Lords are rich, are proud, are obstinate, and they stop the way. (No, and cheers.) Its clergy, who might have led the people and trained them, have given no help. Mr. Simpson very rightly said that it did not matter whether he went to church or not. No; the clergy have been content to take their pay, and care nothing for their flock. (Cheers.) Living they prey on us, and dead they insult us. (Hear, hear.) Living they rob us, and dead they close our graveyards against us. (Hear, hear.) And the representative of the Church here to-day says that 4,400,000 people are not to be reckoned. No; he says, "Oh, yes, I will reckon them—I will reckon some of them into the Church of England." But, if so, his facts are wrong, because he reckoned them as non-worshippers, who did not belong to any body whatever of a religious character, and that is why he left them out, he said. If that was right last night, it must be right to-night; and if it is right to-night, I plead for those nearly 11,000,000 of people who, in 1851, did not belong to the Church. I ask that what was stolen years ago of monastic lands and of tithes, what was taken from the people when the people were not strong, and what has not been devoted to the education and reformation of the people—I ask, not that it should be given to religious bodies, but that it shall be given to educate those who are now ignorant, and to raise those who are now degraded. (Cheers.) I know that the cause of disestablishment might have had here a better advocate than myself to night—(No)—but at least I represent the mass of the people, who are in earnest on this question; and if the Church were a real Church, when it knows that 11,000,000 of people do not want it, it would say : "We abandon the wealth which the law gives us, and we rely on the voluntary aid of our people." (Cheers.) But its Bishops know that they are only like leeches who hang on to the State. There are fat deaneries and cathedral stalls; there are benefices well paid; and, whilst even in their own Church there are poor Curates with threadbare coats, we find the Bishops going for scores of thousands of pounds for the repairs of their palaces, their lean kine growing hungrier every day. (Cheers.) Why do we wish for the disestablishment of the Church? because we want religious equality in this country. - I plead for the expulsion of the Bishops out of the House of Lords, because they kept the taxes on knowledge as long as they dared, kept the tax on paper, and hindered the opening of the school doors : and I plead in the name of education, in the name of the people, against this corrupt institution of the Church of England. (Loud cheers.)

A vote of thanks to the Chairman closed the proceedings.

Printed and Published by C. WATTS, 17, Johnson's Court, Fleet Street London, E.C.

WORKS BY C. BRADLAUGH.

Autobiography of Mr. Bradlaugh	0	3

Political.

Impeachment of the House of Brunswick	1	0
Cromwell and Washington : A Contrast	0	6
Life of George Prince of Wales, with Recent Contrasts and Coincidences	0	2
Letter from a Freemason to Albert Edward, Prince of Wales	0	1
The Land Question (for general distribution)	0	½
Why do Men Starve ?	0	1
Poverty, and its effects on the Political Condition of the People	0	1
Labour's Prayer	0	1
Real Representation of the People (fourth edition)	0	2
American Politics	0	2
The Land, the People, and the Coming Struggle (2nd edition)	0	2
Letter to Dr. Kenealy	0	1
Letter to the Prince of Wales on his Indian Visit	0	1

Theological.

Three Replies to the Three Discourses of the Bishop of Peterborough on Christianity, Scepticism, and Faith	1	0
Heresy : its Morality and Utility	0	9
Six Letters to the Bishop of Lincoln on the Inspiration of the Bible	0	6
When Were our Gospels Written ? A reply to Dr. Tischendorf and the Religious Tract Society	0	6
A Plea for Atheism	0	3
Has Man a Soul ?	0	3
Is there a God ?	0	1
Who was Jesus Christ ?	0	1
What did Jesus Christ Teach.	0	1
The Twelve Apostles	0	1
The Atonement	0	1
New Life of David	0	1
New Life of Jacob	0	1
New Life of Jonah	0	1
Life of Abraham	0	1
Life of Moses	0	1
Were Adam and Eve our First Parents ?	0	1
A Few Words about the Devil	0	1
National Secular Society's Tracts—1. Address to Christians. 2. Who was Jesus ? 7. What is Secularism ? 8. Who are the Secularists ? Per hundred (post free 1s 2d)	1	0
Polemical Essays, Volumes I. and II., each	1	0

Debates.

Two Nights with Mr. Thomas Cooper, on the Being and Attributes of God	0	6
God, Man, and the Bible. Three Nights with the Rev. D. Baylee	0	6
Is there a God ? Two Nights with Alexander Robertson, of Dundonnochie, at Edinburgh. With preface by Austin Holyoake	0	6

Published by C. WATTS, 17, Johnson's Court, Fleet Street, E.C.

www.ingramcontent.com/pod-product-compliance
Lightning Source LLC
Chambersburg PA
CBHW081522040426
42447CB00013B/3312